DATE DUE

DATE DUE		
DE 19 01		
MY 3 02		
NO 1 02		
DEC 11 2002		
MR 25 04		
FE 18 05		
DE 19 08		

Political Traditions in Foreign Policy Series

Kenneth W. Thompson, Editor

The values, traditions, and assumptions undergirding approaches to foreign policy are often crucial in determining the course of a nation's history. Yet, the interconnections between ideas and policy for landmark periods in our foreign relations remain largely unexamined. The intent of this series is to encourage a marriage between political theory and foreign policy. A secondary objective is to identify theorists with a continuing interest in political thought and international relations, both younger scholars and the small group of established thinkers. Only occasionally have scholarly centers and university presses sought to nurture studies in this area. In the 1950s and 1960s the University of Chicago Center for the Study of American Foreign Policy gave emphasis to such inquiries. Since then the subject has not been the focus of any major intellectual center. The Louisiana State University Press and the series editor, from a base at the Miller Center of Public Affairs at the University of Virginia, have organized this series to meet a need that has remained largely unfulfilled since the mid-1960s.

U.S. FOREIGN POLICY
in the TWENTY-FIRST CENTURY

U.S. FOREIGN POLICY
in the TWENTY-FIRST CENTURY

The Relevance of Realism

ROBERT J. MYERS

LOUISIANA STATE UNIVERSITY PRESS
Baton Rouge

Designer: Barbara Neely Bourgoyne
Typeface: Minion
Typesetter: Coghill Composition Co.
Printer and binder: Edwards Brothers, Inc.

The Introduction was first published in different form as "Hans Morgenthau's Realism and Ameri-can Foreign Policy" in *Ethics and International Affairs*, X. Chapter 6 was first published in somewhat different form as "Notes on the Just War Theory: Whose Justice, Which Wars?" in *Ethics and Interna-tional Affairs*, XI. Lines from *Machiavelli in Hell*, by Sebastian de Grazia, copyright © 1989 by Sebas-tian de Grazia, reprinted by permission of Princeton University Press.

Library of Congress Cataloging-in-Publication Data

Myers, Robert John, 1924–
     U.S. foreign policy in the twenty-first century : the relevance of
realism / Robert J. Myers.
        p.   cm.—(Political traditions in foreign policy series)
     Includes bibliographical references and index.
     ISBN 0-8071-2345-5 (alk. paper)
     1. United States—Foreign relations—1989–   2. United States—
Foreign relations—1989–   —Forecasting.   3. Realism.   I. Title.
II. Title: US foreign policy in the twenty-first century.
III. Series.
E840.M94   1999
327.73—dc21   98-50300
                                                          CIP

The paper in this book meets the guidelines for permanence and durability of the Committee on Pro-duction Guidelines for Book Longevity of the Council on Library Resources. ∞

For Elizabeth Watson Myers
Always and Forever

CONTENTS

PREFACE

During the two-thousand-year history of international politics in the West, a variety of efforts have been made to create order out of the chaotic international scene. This requires consideration of the existing international relations state system and how the leaders of the great powers interact, based on three considerations—interest, power, and moral purpose. All international relations problems everywhere can be fruitfully studied in this framework. This approach is called *political realism*.

This triad, straightforward and parsimonious, requires the intervention of a first-class human mind, a statesman-philosopher, to ensure that the goal of international peace and security can be achieved. This general goal is often interrupted by the ambitions of some leaders to reach a dominant or hegemonic position. From an American perspective in this century, the states wishing to reconstitute the general balance of power, the status quo, were Germany and Japan and finally the Soviet Union. Some claim, however, that a mirror image was at work.

The question of moral purpose often arises for Americans in the foreign policy field, sometimes under conditions of stress and nationalism, to the point of becoming moralistic and egoistic, casting suspicion on the moral paradigm altogether. Yet as we trace the long and ongoing history of international politics, we can see that only those powers with goals beyond very limited interests have made their mark and have relevance today. Questions of good and evil, right and wrong, are never far from the minds of the philosophers who have made international politics their preoccupation. This book also considers the Chinese historical framework for interstate relations, which is a blend of hierarchy and realism that the West has been slow to understand.

When foreign affairs are viewed through the realist prism, human nature as revealed through the ages, at all times and in all societies, is seen to be the foundation of realism. From the Judeo-Christian religious perspective, the human individual, born in sin, is imperfect and will always be so. This idea has an important implication for political action, namely, that while one may strive for good results, they are often flawed in the process. In this century, Reinhold Niebuhr made a deep imprint on our minds, cautioning that the "lesser evil" was the best we could expect. This conclusion does not, however, discourage crusaders. To fill in the gap between what is and what might be in this system, utopian models have arisen periodically, claiming the sighting of a new era in international relations as though it were a new comet.

How realism has dealt with these challenges and where it stands today as a model for international relations are the subject of this book. In addition to utopian critics, there are those who would improve realism itself—such as Michael W. Doyle, whose recent book *Ways of War and Peace* (New York: Norton, 1997) divides realists into four camps and presents idealists in two categories, liberals and socialists. One of the overarching concerns of this study is how well the realist system has held up and what can be expected of it in the future.

On 24 July 1997 in Los Angeles, U.S. secretary of state Madeleine Albright concluded her speech on Southeast Asia as follows: "We have a responsibility in our time, as others have had in theirs, not to be prisoners of history, but to shape history; a responsibility to play the role of the pathfinder, to join in constructing a global network of purpose and law that will protect our citizens, defend our interests and preserve our values for the remaining years of this century and through the next." It is not difficult to see in that statement the triad of interest, power, and moral purpose.

This project began shortly after I became president of the Carnegie Council on Ethics and International Affairs in New York City in 1980. In that position, of course, I was confronted with the ethical aspects of politics; America's preoccupation with morality, the "city on the hill," the desire to institutionalize and defang conflicts through such structures as the United Nations, and other such concerns occupied my time. A longtime friend, Kenneth W. Thompson, director of the Miller Center of Public Affairs at the University of Virginia, first encouraged me to write a book on this general subject.

In this process, I relied on many conversations with Joel H. Rosenthal, now president of the Carnegie Council, who read and improved the manuscript. Another early supporter was Michael Joseph Smith, who advanced the project considerably by allowing me to teach his course in ethics and statecraft during the fall of 1992 and the summer of 1993 at the University of Virginia. The programs and activities of the Carnegie Council through 1994 were of practical help in refining my views, I hope in a coherent and persuasive manner.

Deserving a special mention is Russell Hardin, chair of the political science department at New York University, who spent most of 1997 in residence at the Institute of Advanced Behavioral Sciences at Stanford University. He read and critiqued the manuscript and was always available to discuss political philosophy.

Since leaving the Carnegie Council at the end of 1994, I have been a research fellow at the Hoover Institution at Stanford University. I have benefited by the support of the director, John Raisian, as well as the advice of senior fellows Thomas A. Metzger and Ramon H. Myers on the Chinese worldview. Dr. Metzger's insights on Immanuel Kant were also helpful to me. Adrienne Bronfeld of the Hoover staff gave invaluable attention to the final preparation of the manuscript. Matt Mattern of the Carnegie Council also made an important professional contribution. Errors and misinterpretations in this text are my exclusive responsibility.

Finally, I wish to thank Dean Marsh McCall for offering me a class on ethics and statecraft in the continuing studies program at Stanford. This class has allowed me for the past three years to talk in a regular forum to real students and other citizens about the antinomies of our international condition.

U.S. FOREIGN POLICY
in the TWENTY-FIRST CENTURY

Introduction: The Pattern of U.S. Foreign Policy

With the millennium almost upon us, we can sense a wave of excitement and anticipation that a new era is surely at hand—including a new era of foreign policy and international relations. Whatever the issues of international relations may be, they will be susceptible to solution for no other reason than that there will be new dates on the calendar. One of my objectives in this review and projection of American foreign policy is to consider the limits of change and continuity.

The conduct of foreign policy in America is still highly conditioned by the founding of the country as a revolution against the old order, represented by Great Britain and the political intrigues of the Europeans, both dynastic and religious, that made war a perennial occupation. It was to escape this hubris that America decided on another course: an ideal, almost idyllic, escape from foreign intervention and intrigue, a new world protected by the Atlantic and with a philosophy set in George Washington's "Farewell Address" of 17 September 1796:

> The great rule of conduct for us, in regard to foreign Nations is, in extending our commercial relations, to have with them as little *Political* connection as possible—so far as we have already formed engagements, let them be fulfilled with perfect good faith—Here let us stop. 'Tis our true policy to steer clear of permanent alliances with any portion of the foreign world. Our detached and distant situation invites and enables us to pursue a different course—If we remain one People, under an efficient government, the period is not far off, when we may defy material injury from external annoyance; when we may take such an attitude as will cause the neutrality we may at any time resolve upon to be scrupulously respected.[1]

1. *Letters and Papers of George Washington* (New York: Sun Dial Classics Co., 1909), 400.

Washington distinguished between the foreign and the domestic, the latter being the good, the fulfillment of the domestic dream of equality in freedom by a country under God's blessing. The new nation had a foreordained vision of the new Jerusalem, the "city on the hill," the exceptionalist country.[2] America was inner-directed, destined to realize its unique potential as outlined in the *Federalist* papers, the Declaration of Independence, and the Constitution. In foreign affairs, it would have as few noncommercial relations as possible with foreign countries, which were viewed as both threatening and corrupting this virgin state that was developing its own God-given character and already possessed a sense of its destiny. In this context, foreign relations were rightly considered an infringement on the purpose of America to be a new society and to regard foreign entanglements as an intrusion on the unfettered march to a manifest destiny in North America.

In brief, there was an early American distrust of and aversion to international relations as a marginal and uncomfortable idea—that just as American individualism was self-evidently self-sufficient, so was the American collective, the federal nation. This condition was a product of its manner of settlement, a unique phenomenon in an otherwise reckless world of Europeans. The founders were well aware of the dangers surrounding them. Men endlessly pursued power, motivated, as Thucydides, the Greek historian of the Peloponnesian War, put it, by "honor, fear and, interest." America hoped to avoid this reality in world affairs by holding foreign powers at arm's length.[3]

By the mid-nineteenth century, hardened by the War of 1812 and the rise and fall of Napoleon as the principal European events, and ravaged by the Civil War, America had developed a conviction of continental sufficiency, rather than international imperium. The Civil War settled the issue of federalism, at least until the end of the next century. The martial urge was moderated by the growing belief in inevitable progress, based on the evidence of scientific advance and the appeals of religion and industry for a peaceful future. These influences are still with us.

The Belle Epoque toward the end of the nineteenth century resonated across the Atlantic. (Contrary to this trend was the U.S. imperial foray against Spain, mediation of the Russo-Japanese War, and Teddy Roosevelt's "great white

---

2. For a recent treatment of this historic theme, see Seymour Martin Lipset, *American Exceptionalism: A Double-Edged Sword* (New York: Norton, 1996).

3. The role of power in the American Revolutionary War, however, has been explored by Theodore Draper in *A Struggle for Power: The American Revolution* (New York: Times Books/Random House, 1996).

fleet," which increased America's capability to become involved in international affairs.) War in Europe seemed to have been rendered obsolete because of the rise of international commerce, the growing solidarity of the working class, and the rise of military technology. Further, the leading powers—Germany, England, and the United States—shared the same religion, so surely war could be avoided, an insight articulated by Andrew Carnegie. But what followed was an extraordinary series of international catastrophes—World War I, World War II, and then almost fifty years of the Cold War. This series of events could hardly escape the notice of the political leaders who had envisioned the quite different scenario of the Belle Epoque, but the consequences somehow were muted.[4]

This is not to say that after each of these disasters no one came forward with recommendations and various action plans, or that the balance of power was completely forgotten in the chaos of international anarchy. The League of Nations was the primary response to World War I, to try to make the world safe for democracy, even though Woodrow Wilson was unable to persuade America to join in this undertaking. Yet the Wilsonian effort to create a world governed by a comity of nations left an uncertain order, a dream to be fulfilled. As Peter Rodman has stated, "Wilson was the father of modern American internationalism and world leadership, the pioneer vindicated by the disaster of isolation in the 1920's, all the more heroic for the tragic failure he had suffered in his own time."[5] The ideal dimmed in the international politics of the 1930s, which seemed to flounder on empty rhetoric and futile legalisms.[6] Adolf Hitler's alliance with the Soviet Union and the combined attack on Poland showed the hand of naked power.

The aftermath of World War II produced the United Nations, which will be discussed in more detail later. But some saw this mechanistic, legalistic approach to the problem of international conflict and the struggle for power as lacking in practicality. And out of this argument against high-minded aspirations and idealism arose a counterargument, speaking plainly and unambiguously of the need to forgo utopia, which had always been an illusion, for an honest appreciation of the fundamentals of international relations. This was the

4. See Eric Hobsbawm, *The Age of Extremes: A History of the World, 1914–1991* (New York: Pantheon, 1994).

5. Peter Rodman, *More Precious Than Peace* (New York: Charles Scribner's Sons, 1994), 6. For a full treatment of the Wilsonian quest for a new world order, see Thomas J. Knock, *To End All Wars: Woodrow Wilson and the Quest for a New World Order* (Princeton: Princeton University Press, 1992).

6. See E. H. Carr, *The Twenty Years' Crisis, 1919–1939: An Introduction to the Study of International Relations* (London: Macmillan, 1942).

old European experience of running a world of sovereign states, the model aris-ing to meet Thomas Hobbes's *Leviathan,* with close attention to power and in-terests and the careful balancing of these factors. It was finally the articulation of this tradition in America, defined as realism, that provided an intellectual basis for the foreign policy that brought the West through the Cold War and is now in dispute among revisionists. Henry Kissinger expresses the U.S. foreign policy dichotomy succinctly: "The singularities that America has ascribed to it-self throughout its history have produced two contradictory attitudes toward foreign policy. The first is that America serves its values best by perfecting de-mocracy at home, thereby acting as a beacon for the rest of mankind, the sec-ond, that America's values impose on it obligations to crusade for them around the world. Torn between nostalgia for a pristine past and yearning for a perfect future, American thought has oscillated between isolationism and commit-ment, though since the end of the Second World War the realities of interde-pendence have predominated."[7] But there remained no agreement on the pa-rameters for American foreign policy conduct and prognosis, or on why the real problem may be the subject matter as well as our self-limitations. Expectations outrun the realities.

And what are these expectations? One polarity is the idealist one, which ex-pects international competition to be settled through open negotiations charac-terized by goodwill and self-sacrifice. Power considerations are marginalized. Realists, in contrast, doubt that significant issues can be handled so easily, that the side with the ability to leverage its power will obtain an agreement in its in-terest. The realist position, however, does not exclude the possibility of reci-procity in critical issues. The purpose of this book on international politics is to restate the possible outcomes of this familiar tension so that there may be a broader consensus on what we can expect and accept about how the political world works in both "normal" times and "times of crisis." It will include an ap-praisal of the moral, or human, condition as one of the central factors in state-craft, reflecting what exists as well as what might be in the international com-munity.

This effort, then, is a restatement of realism, a somewhat battered term, against the agenda of reform or revolution that periodically shakes the litera-ture—but not the conduct—of foreign policy. The claim here is not that this is the only way to look at international politics, but rather that, based on history

---

7. Henry Kissinger, *Diplomacy* (New York: Simon & Schuster, 1994), 18.

and human nature, it is the most instructive. We need to assert what is permanent and what is contingent about realism.[8]

The realist-idealist distinction was the primary argument in the immediate post–World War II period. (Competing explanations, such as neorealism and rational choice, had not yet come on the scene.) Hans J. Morgenthau, for example, was convinced that international relations was the critical issue of the day, and he reluctantly dedicated his talents and energies to this subject (actually preferring philosophy), realizing that if Soviet power was not balanced, freedom would be lost, possibly in radioactive rubble.[9] Rallying the West against this threat through rapid rearmament was the immediate goal. Idealism seemed blind to this menace, and its reliance on such ideas as collective security through the United Nations and goodwill toward the Soviet Union, which was gobbling up Eastern Europe, seemed to deal recklessly with the national interest.

Morgenthau felt obligated to develop a theory of realism to guide international politics. This theory was based on interest, power, and morality. This triad created the foundation for the view of a perduring human nature, which runs through the realist interpretation of politics. It is also dependent on the statesman, on human volition, to weigh variables in constructing the "national interest." Providing more specifics and clarification was the later self-appointed task of the neorealists, who wished to improve the realist program by studying the growing international structures in their proliferation and complexity, to delineate "regimes" that kept these structures in motion. Some of the leading contributors to this school of internationalism have been Robert O. Keohane, Joseph S. Nye, Jr., and Kenneth N. Waltz.[10]

Another school, seeking not to improve realism but to replace it altogether, is from a branch of rational choice. Drawing an analogue from economics, rational choice international relations theorists seek to maximize the actor's prospects in any given situation by the pursuit of his rational best interests, setting up models for trade-offs based on mathematical formulas. If this idea is valid in economics, its proponents argue, then it is also valid in other social sciences, including international politics.

8. See Kenneth W. Thompson, *Understanding World Politics* (Notre Dame, Ind.: University of Notre Dame Press, 1975).

9. See Kenneth W. Thompson and Robert J. Myers, eds., *Truth and Tragedy* (New Brunswick: Transaction Books, 1984) 381.

10. See, for example, Robert O. Keohane, *Neorealism and Its Critics* (New York: Columbia University Press, 1986).

On this question, Morgenthau was emphatic: rational choice in international politics is simply another utopia. He summarizes critics of this persuasion as follows:

> In the aftermath of World War II, reflections on international relations entered an entirely new phase. This phase is marked by a number of academic schools of thought—behaviorism, systems analysis, game theory, simulation, and methodology in general—that have one aim in common: the pervasive rationalization of international relations by means of a comprehensive theory. The ultimate purpose is still practical: to increase the stability of prediction and thereby remove uncertainty from political action. Yet this practicality is different from the traditional kind. The latter endeavored to maximize rationality and success through the rational manipulation of the objective factors of international relations, the former attempts to eradicate obstacles to pervasive rationalizations that are inherent in the objective character of international relations by overwhelming them with theoretical devices. The new theories, insofar as they are new in more than terminology, are in truth not so much theories as dogmas. They do not so much try to reflect reality as it actually is as to superimpose upon a reluctant reality a theoretical scheme that satisfies the desire for thorough rationalization. Their practicality is specious, since it substitutes what is desirable for what is possible. The new theories are in truth utopias, differing from the utopians of old only in that they replace the simple and obvious deductions from ethical postulates with a highly complex and sophisticated methodological and terminological apparatus, creating the illusion of demonstration.[11]

Debate over the validity of looking at the world through the realist telescope goes on unabated. The realist core, however, in my view, holds up remarkably well. As Ethan Kapstein says, "In order to overthrow a theory, one needs a new theory that does a better job of explaining both the old observations and the new observations. Part and parcel of the falsification process is alternative theory."[12] A 1972 survey found that the "overwhelming majority" of postwar general theorists work in the realist tradition.[13]

---

11. Hans J. Morgenthau, *Truth and Power: Essays of a Decade, 1960–70* (New York: Praeger, 1970), 242–43. For a potent critique of rational choice in political science, see Donald P. Green and Ian Shapiro, *Pathologies of Rational Choice Theory: A Critique of Applications in Political Science* (New Haven: Yale University Press, 1994); for a more felicitous outcome for rational choice partisans, see Russell Hardin, *One for All: The Logic of Group Conflict* (Princeton: Princeton University Press, 1995).

12. Ethan Kapstein, "Is Realism Dead? The Democratic Sources of International Politics," *IO, International Organization* 49 (Autumn 1995): 758. Also see Charles W. Kegley, Jr., ed., *Controversies in International Relations Theory: Realism and the Neoliberal Challenge* (New York: St. Martin's Press, 1995).

13. See Michael Doyle, *Ways of War and Peace* (New York: Norton, 1997), 41n.

Another contemporary observation on the strength of the realist tradition is from Robert Kagan, in an article that levels criticism at some points of realist theory. "The realist central insights into the competitive and conflictual nature of mankind remain true; nor should we forget the truism that all great powers must some day fall. Indeed, the task of realism should be to warn us that the present happy state of affairs is extremely fragile; we live in an interwar period. But how long that period will last, and what quality of international life can be achieved in the interim, are matters which Americans hold it in their power to influence."[14]

The conduct of foreign policy is conservative in both style and substance for very good reasons. Interests tend to change slowly, short of some technological triumph or other revolutionary innovation. While society as a whole is subject to continuing change, the bedrock of realism depends on the constancy of relevant aspects of human nature for its ability to compare historical developments against a norm, putting forward self-interest, power, and morality as the essential foundation. If we review the salient claims of historical realist philosophy, we find only those three fundamental points: the immutable facts of self-interest, the struggle for power, and the inevitable involvement of morality in political decision making and political action, whether the actor wishes it so or not. Even Immanuel Kant notes the problem of conflict and struggle in society: "Man wishes concord, but nature knowing better what is good for his species, wishes discord."[15] One can speculate that his view of human nature contributed to his hope for the cure of institutional change as a way out of this dilemma.

Self-interest, an element that cannot be automatically taken for granted as rational, ideally controls power, so that power is harnessed by a rational self-interest. The political leader then uses this tool for a good purpose, a moral purpose, a normative end worthy of his (or her) statecraft. This three-part system can be described as a "theory" of politics, imprecise as a theory involving politics and human beings must be; or one might simply call it an "approach" to international politics; or, as another writer puts it, "A theory of international relations can only be a set of generalities about the whole of international relations, and not merely its parts."[16]

---

14. Robert Kagan, "American Power: A Guide for the Perplexed," *Commentary* 101 (April 1996): 30.

15. Immanuel Kant, *Religion within the Limits of Reason Alone*, VIII, 21. A discussion of Kant and international relations is in Chapter 3.

16. Kyung Won Kim, *Revolution and International System* (New York: New York University Press, 1970), ii.

There is no escaping a "theory" of politics. The theory provides a paradigm of how politics is performing in society. Its telos is the best policy outcome available. When the outcome is flawed, then it is the task of theory to point out what went wrong. Or as Kenneth W. Thompson says, "The task of theory is to an important degree one of the abstracting from the total reality some part which may permit the study and examination of living problems. This abstraction remains one aspect of international relations from its total context, whether it is power, interest or community. There is merit in this approach, at the same time that it runs the risk of all abstractions. A vigorous debate on the issues of theory may serve the purpose of separating meaningless abstractions from those that have usefulness."[17] So a selective theory is possible; it will not come in a scientific way (that is, it cannot be duplicated precisely, as in the physical and natural sciences), but it does contain a usable truth. This is all one can expect of the social sciences. Positivism, on the other hand, seeks to assert a single scientific method, applicable to the natural and physical as well as "social" sciences.[18]

Ideally, says Thompson, "the organized body of facts and knowledge upon which the theorist must depend spans the limits of human knowledge." Since no single person is likely to accumulate that knowledge in a lifetime, one looks to history (and psychology) for examples of success in interstate relations, both ancient and contemporary, and does the best one can to "theorize" about international relations. This can provide only one answer—not the whole answer—but it is my contention that realism presents the best available explanation for international relations. Peter Parent has suggested that the roles of theory are utilitarian, cognitive, and pedagogic. Our interest here is utilitarian.[19]

As I have stated, interest, power, and morality compose the key elements of Morgenthau's theory of international relations. In the first edition of his book *Politics among Nations,* he had not yet seen the need to enunciate a theory of international relations as such. At that juncture, he relied on inductive examples in history and other empirical observations. He believed that the world had changed after World War II in two fundamental ways: first, the United States, although the world's most powerful nation, was no longer viewed as omnipotent but could be threatened by enemies, and second, modern technology (i.e.,

17. Thompson, *Understanding World Politics,* 180.

18. Also see Mark A. Neufeld, *The Restructuring of International Relations Theory* (New York: Cambridge University Press, 1995), Chap. 2.

19. See Peter Parent, "The Genesis of War," introduction to Carl von Clausewitz, *On War,* ed. and trans. Michael Howard and Peter Parent (Princeton: Princeton University Press, 1984), 578.

nuclear weapons) raised the possibility of total war and the destruction of civilization.[20] He organized this work around two concepts, power and peace, setting the polarities that distinguished the book.

Despite the book's popular and intellectual success, Morgenthau was disappointed, even angered, by some of the criticism it occasioned. He discusses this problem in a new preface to the second edition, where he complains that he has been criticized for ideas he never expressed or even held. Exactly what those were are detailed in the preface to the third edition: "I am still being told that I believe in the prominence of the international system based upon the nation state, although the obsolescence of the nation state and the need to merge it into supranational organizations of a functional nature was already one of the main points of the first edition of 1948. I am still being told that I am making success the standard of political action. Even so, as far back as 1955 I refuted that conception of politics with the same arguments which are being used against me. And, of course, I am still being accused of indifference to the moral problem in spite of abundant evidence in this book and elsewhere, to the contrary."[21]

Raising up and analyzing Morgenthau's work as a point of departure does not mean ignoring the contributions and distinctions made by a variety of twentieth-century realists as well as a long line of historical predecessors, who will be referred to as appropriate. But for the purpose of my thesis and of relating realism to contemporary and future U.S. foreign policy, it is sufficient to concentrate on Morgenthau's work and his theory as the father of the realist school.[22] Although Morgenthau's views are well received in many quarters, both he and his realist companions—such as E. H. Carr, Walter Lippmann, George Kennan, Robert Gilpin, Henry Kissinger, and Kenneth W. Thompson—still are criticized for adhering to realism in their analyses of international relations. Some of the complaints are from small states, powerless to make much of a contribution to the current system, and some are from those who would adopt

20. Hans J. Morgenthau, *Politics among Nations: The Struggle for Power and Peace* (New York: Knopf, 1948), 8.

21. Morgenthau, *Politics among Nations*, 3d ed. (New York: Knopf, 1960), preface.

22. See, for example, Stanley Hoffmann's review of the sixth edition (1985) of *Politics among Nations*, revised by Kenneth W. Thompson (New York: Knopf, 1985), in the *Atlantic Monthly* 56 (November 1985): 131–36; Joel H. Rosenthal, *Righteous Realists: Political Realism, Responsible Power, and American Culture in the Nuclear Age* (Baton Rouge: Louisiana State University Press, 1991); and Michael Joseph Smith, *Realism from Weber to Kissinger* (Baton Rouge: Louisiana State University Press, 1986).

criteria other than power, interest, and morality but have difficulty coming up with a better alternative.

The original edition of *Politics among Nations* began with a chapter titled "International Politics: A Dual Approach." First, the reader was urged to "understand international politics" through careful study and historical analogy, and to be wary of misplaced parallels and skeptical of prophecy. Contradictory traditions are often at work, "but what tendency actually will prevail is anybody's guess."[23] Before writing *Politics among Nations,* Morgenthau had no firsthand experience in either politics or diplomacy, but the book was his entrée into various consultancies in both the State and Defense Departments until 1965 and his break with the Johnson administration over Vietnam. In Cold War terms, he was a hard-liner, and the book as it stood was his red badge of courage.

The second edition was revised to meet criticism of the first. Morgenthau added a new first chapter on theory, which stressed six points. Three of these points were philosophically enduring, while the other three were descriptive and subject to change and modification. Like everyone else, he recognized that conditions change (although human nature does not).[24] The most significant addition to his theory was the unequivocal recognition of the moral dimension of realism.[25] He had dealt extensively with morality and politics in his first book, *Scientific Man vs. Power Politics,*[26] and had included considerations of ethics and morals in the first edition of *Politics among Nations.* His enunciation of the theory made it henceforth impossible to discuss Morgenthau and international politics without referring to ethics, even though there were some who preferred to think of ethics as outside the realm of international relations theory.[27] Over the years since the 1950s, however, not only has that connection been vindicated but it remains in the forefront of serious discussions on the subject. The necessity of having a theory at all to consider international relations, as opposed to some guiding principles or assumptions, is another matter.

23. Morgenthau, *Politics among Nations,* 1st ed., 6.

24. See, for example, Verlyn Klinkenborg, "We Are Still Only Human: For Better and Worse, Human Nature Remains Constant," *New York Times Magazine,* 1 September 1996.

25. A valuable, but curious, article, "The Moral Politics of Hans Morgenthau," by A. J. H. Murray, claims an overlooked discovery of morality in Morgenthau's ethics, based on that of Saint Augustine, in *Review of Politics* 58 (1996): 81–107.

26. Hans J. Morgenthau, *Scientific Man vs. Power Politics* (Chicago: University of Chicago Press, 1946).

27. See a refutation of this point by the author in the introduction to Vol. 1 of *Ethics and International Affairs* (1987).

University of Chicago professor Leo Strauss, one of the readers of the new first chapter, commented that he saw no more need for a theory of international relations than for a theory of plumbing. Nonetheless, there is no shortage of books on international relations theory.[28] Martin Wight divides the theorists into three schools—realists, who concentrate on the problem of international anarchy; rationalists, who prefer functions, law, and institution building; and revolutionaries, who would turn the system of sovereign national states into some variety of world government. Another valuable book in this regard is Robert L. Rothstein's *Evolution of Theory in International Relations.*[29] Theory is needed to critique performance.

Doyle is critical of the classical theorists because "some of what [they] discovered is dated, since they failed to articulate key aspects of the political universe we inhabit today. None of the theorists examined here anticipated the destructiveness of nuclear weapons or the speed of global communications."[30] This, in my view, confuses philosophy with technology.[31]

Morgenthau's theory begins modestly enough:

> This book purports to present a theory of international politics. Its validity is to be tested both empirically and logically. In short, is the theory consistent with the facts and within itself. . . . The issue that this theory raises concerns the nature of all politics. The history of modern political thought is the story of a contest between two schools that differ fundamentally in their conception of the nature of man, society, and politics. One believes that a rational and moral political order, derived from universally valid abstract principles, can be achieved here and now. It assumes the essential goodness and infinite malleability of human nature, and blames the failure of the social order to measure up to rational standards on lack of knowledge and understanding, obsolescent social institutions, or the depravity of certain isolated individuals or groups. It trusts in education, reform, and the sporadic use of force to remedy these defects.[32]

The other theory, or point of view, standing in opposition to this conception of man and politics, "believes that the world, imperfect as it is from the rational

28. Charles R. Beitz, *Political Theory and International Relations* (Princeton: Princeton University Press, 1979); Kenneth Waltz, *Man, the State, and War: A Theoretical Analysis* (New York: Columbia University Press, 1959); and Martin Wight, *International Theory: The Three Traditions* (New York: Holmes & Meier, 1992).

29. Robert L. Rothstein, ed., *The Evolution of Theory in International Relations* (Columbia: University of South Carolina Press, 1991).

30. Doyle, *Ways of War and Peace,* 9.

31. See Donald Kagan, *On the Origins of War and the Preservation of Peace* (New York: Doubleday, 1995), 3.

32. Morgenthau, *Politics among Nations,* 3.

point of view, is the result of forces inherent in human nature. To improve the world, one must work with those forces, not against them. This being inherently a world of opposing interests, and of conflict among them, moral principles can never be fully realized, but must at least be approximated through the ever temporary balancing of interests and the ever precarious settlement of conflicts. This school, then, sees in a system of checks and balances a universal principle for all pluralistic societies. It appeals to historic precedent rather than to abstract principles, and aims at the realization of the lesser evil rather than the absolute good."[33]

Morgenthau's first point is that there are objective laws rooted in human nature, which determine the operation of society in general. From this perspective, one distinguishes truth from mere opinion and works in harmony with human nature rather than opposing it.[34] The essence of human nature Morgenthau finds in the classical historical past, in China, India, and Greece, adding that "novelty is not necessarily a virtue in political theory, nor is old age a defect." He concludes, not without irony, that "the fact that a theory of politics, *if there is such a theory*, has never been heard of before, tends to create a presumption against, rather than in favor of, its soundness. Conversely, the fact that a theory of politics was developed hundreds or even thousands of years ago—as was the theory of the balance of power—does not create a presumption that it must be outmoded and obsolete. A theory of politics must be subjected to the dual tests of reason and experience."[35] Facts must be weighed and integrated by reason, which allows these facts to come alive according to the situation. This is the first of the three enduring points.

Morgenthau then proceeds to his second point, the concept of "interest defined in terms of power." He sees this as the link "between reason trying to understand international politics and the facts to be understood." This creates an autonomous sphere of politics, Morgenthau asserts, and, after Aristotle, he mentions similar claims for economics, ethics, aesthetics, and religion. One can only speculate why politics (power) has not been considered as an autonomous phenomenon before; it is not that others have ignored the subject of power. "To be visible, power most relate to something, either people or 'dead matter.' . . . the chief cause of change in the modern world is the increased power over matter that we owe to science."[36] One can accept Morgenthau's claim, although

33. Ibid., 4.

34. Cf. a similar discussion in Eiji Uehiro, *Practical Ethics for You* (Tokyo: Jinri Press, 1986), 24–27.

35. Morgenthau, *Politics among Nations*, 4; emphasis added.

36. See, for example, Bertrand Russell, *Power: A New Social Analysis* (New York: Norton, 1938).

I find it difficult. I can think of religion and aesthetics, for example, as self-contained ideas, illuminating themselves internally and affecting one's sensibilities in one direction or another. It may be that power is so interconnected (actor-subject) that it cannot be productively considered only in its own sphere but rather must be analyzed in terms of its consequences. This notion, however, shatters the idea of its autonomy and releases it into the struggle for power in society at large, which seems to be a more appropriate setting to consider its complexities and outcomes. A view of power as nonautonomous seems to be more in line with the idea of human nature's concentration on power, self-interest, and morality. What one gains in analytical insight through the concept of the autonomy of power is something of a mystery. Morgenthau claims this is the way statesmen always think, but reading memoirs of statesmen and generals reveals a more nuanced weighing of all relevant factors—and on occasion, appalling oversights—as constituting the motive of power. Power gains its force and relevance from its connection with other empirical factors. The second enduring point is "interest defined as power."[37] Whether power can be dealt with as an autonomous matter, finally, is not necessary to the argument.

The third point is a simple and acceptable assertion that "realism does not endorse a key concept of interest defined as power with a meaning that is fixed once and for all." George Washington's "Farewell Address" is a good case in point. In other words, historical and cultural factors influence the meaning of interest defined as power and how that force might be applied. Morgenthau states: "Power may comprise anything that establishes and maintains the control of man over man. This power covers all social relationships which serve that end, from physical violence to the most subtle psychological ties by which one mind controls another." Morgenthau even reduced this idea to the family level, in a moment of levity, on how to deal with a mother-in-law. The card game three-handed hearts is another familiar example. Further, "Political realism does not assume that the contemporary conditions under which foreign policy operates, with their extreme instability and the ever present threat of large-scale violence, cannot be changed. The balance of power, for instance, is indeed a perennial element of all pluralistic societies, as the authors of *The Federalist* papers well knew; yet it is capable of operating as it does in the United States, under the conditions of relative stability and peaceful conflict. If these factors can be duplicated in the international sphere, then international politics can be transformed."[38]

37. Ibid., 136.
38. Morgenthau, *Politics among Nations*, 3d ed., 9.

It is important to realize that this transformation occurs by working with the forces of the actual world, that is, interest, power, and morality, rather than depending on some ideal world community to create a new order. Discovering mutual interests, areas of compromise, is essential. In Morgenthau's view, realism is the only reliable way to bring about appropriate change in the operation of international relations, encompassing as it does both technological potentialities and moral requirements. This is Morgenthau's answer to his critics who say he ignores the possibility of change because of his position on the immutable character of human nature; rather, he sees change occurring all the time in the objective conditions of society, filtered through the constant of human nature. This is a useful observation, but it is not central to the core of my argument for realist theory.

This leads to Morgenthau's fourth and probably most controversial point on the role of morality in politics. This subject will be considered in subsequent chapters, especially when we turn to Thucydides, Machiavelli, and Kant, and take a look at the Chinese worldview. "Political realism is aware," he wrote, "of the moral significance of political action. It is also aware of the ineluctable tension between the moral command and the requirements of successful political action. And it is unwilling to gloss over and obliterate that tension and thus to obfuscate both the moral and the political issue by making it appear as though the stark facts of politics were morally more satisfying than they actually are, and the moral law less exacting than it actually is."[39] Like Reinhold Niebuhr, Morgenthau cast the decision-making process, the moral choice, in terms of the anguish of power, knowing that all political action is evil. (This raises questions of "right" versus "good" that occur from taking the Niebuhrian position on political action.) Immanuel Kant, proclaiming the superiority of principle over consequences, urged his followers to pursue their principles, even if it meant that the world would perish. This might be an appropriate stance for an individual martyr, but the statesman is driven by the higher universal moral principles of the protection of one's citizens and the survival of the state. Freedom is also a universal moral principle, yet on occasion, it will be waived in favor of survival, for example, the surrender of Luxembourg to the Nazis in World War II. Morgenthau presumably added the particular focus on his personal awareness of moral concerns as an answer to critics who charged him with an unswerving priority on power for its own sake. In *Scientific Man vs. Power Politics*, he eschews the usual and convenient distinction between private and public

---

39. Ibid., 10.

morality in favor of a single standard.[40] This position, however, he often aban-
dons in his textbook and other books and articles—but never his insistence on
the inevitable connection of morality with political choice. This is the third pillar of the core realist position.

Morgenthau's fifth point is a warning against the hubris of nations that project their own interests and image on the international scene, proclaiming their
pride and superiority. The United States, in its appeal to "exceptionalism," always stands in danger of taking such a risk. "Political realism refuses to identify
the moral aspiration of a particular nation with the moral laws that govern the
universe." During the Cold War, both the USSR and the United States launched
competing claims to that effect, and the new competitor for the United States is
already at hand, that is, China, with a different worldview as well (see Chapter
4). "There is a world of difference between the belief that all nations stand
under the judgment of God, inscrutable to the human mind, and the blasphemous conviction that God is always on one's side and that what one wills cannot fail to be willed by God also."[41] It is this latter belief and operating principle
among nations that seriously challenges the legitimacy of the "just war," a subject that will also be considered in a later chapter.

A more significant point here, however, is whether this caution on a "crusading foreign policy" is relevant for the United States. Morgenthau was concerned
that if ideology, that of both the Soviet Union and the United States—rather
than the prudent national interest—led the conduct of foreign policy, it would
mean endless wars of a quasi-religious character, such as befell medieval Europe
and inflict the Middle East today. Wilsonian projects, such as making the world
safe for democracy, aroused Morgenthau's concern. Today, however, with
much of the world apparently moving in a general democratic direction and the
Clinton administration's embrace of "enlargement" of democracy and free
markets as the center of its foreign policy, one might consider revising this in-
junction (see the concluding chapter).

Because of these five principles, Morgenthau as his sixth point claims that his
theory of realism is profoundly different from that of other schools. Clearly he
separates it from idealism in more detail than he did in his opening paragraphs.
He is convinced that these principles establish an autonomous sphere of politics. Yet one senses the weakness and ambivalence of such a position and wonders why it is not enough to assert the primacy of political thought when dealing with political matters, without excluding other relevant inputs that come

40. Morgenthau, *Scientific Man vs. Power Politics*, 178–79.
41. Morgenthau, *Politics among Nations*, 3d ed., 11.

from other (and not really autonomous) worlds to balance one's judgment. Almost four of the twelve pages devoted to the theory are on this sixth point, all exhorting (and yet defending) the autonomy argument. Take "religious man," for example:

> To understand "religious man," I must for the time being abstract from the other aspects of human nature and deal with its religious aspect as if it were the only one. Furthermore, I must apply to the religious sphere the standards of thought appropriate to it, *always remaining aware of the existence of other standards and their actual influence upon the religious qualities of man.* What is true of this facet of human nature is true of all the others. No modern economist, for instance, would conceive of his science and its relations to other sciences of man in any other way. It is exactly through such a process of emancipation from single standards of thought, and the development of one appropriate to its subject matter, that economics has developed as an autonomous theory of the economic activities of man. To contribute to a similar development in the field of politics is indeed the purpose of political realism.

Morgenthau concludes that such a theory and the consequent foreign policy will "not meet with unanimous approval. One reason is the disparagement of power in contemporary society, and the other the need for self-deception to make palatable playing a role in politics."[42] Yet our theory of realism is not dependent in any way on the autonomy argument; a primacy is sufficient.

Although it is true that realist arguments did not persuade idealists that something much better must be around the corner, the Cold War years saw a strong adherence to realist principles, including the moral claim, particularly in the insistence that there was no moral equivalence between the values of the West and those of the Soviet Union and its adherents. Moral questions, as they must be, were an integral part of the Cold War facedown. To be sure, at the same time there were realists who were opposed to the inclusion of morality as a gravitas in weighing international decision making, not realizing that realpolitik without an end justification of a moral nature would not work; the idealists fretted over the presumed limiting possibilities imposed by the human nature paradigm of self-interest, power, and morality. As for morality, some statesmen cite a "higher duty" in the realm of transcendental obligations as well as the Weberian ethic of "responsibility," which avoids moral judgment by claiming the exclusive duty of consequences. Even the "national interest" is subject to this array of criticisms, if it is not defined in moral terms.

---

42. Ibid., 14; emphasis added.

In this context, Kenneth Thompson makes a strong statement for the realist case: "Realism approaches international politics in the same way it approaches human relations as the arena where self-pride and self-interest commingle with high purposes. Man is a curious and contradictory blending of selfishness and virtue. Philosophers who talk only of more selfishness fail to explain how we are able to recognize self-centeredness in the absence of virtue and concern for others."[43]

It is well that the realist-idealist dialogue continues in modern politics and in academe, as well as in the United Nations and its many functional affiliates. Better understanding and performance are essential elements in handling power well in the successful pursuit of a good political end, that is to say, how to use power for the maximum good and the minimum evil. The outcome, however, is not always obvious or unambiguous; arguments over means selected and their application to a specific end of politics are the stuff of political debate and often acrimony. Any exercise of power toward the actor's ends invariably erodes others' positions or shatters their illusion of autonomy. This is what we mean by the corrupting influence of power, either on the actor or on the object or both.

In international politics, for example, a case of intervention into another country for whatever purpose sets off a chain of events that has unknowable consequences. (See Chapter 6 on just war arguments on intervention.) Statesmen are often judged by their citizens on how well they anticipate particular consequences to justify the initial measures and their projected outcome. An ideal result might be politically astute, the end achieved, and morally proper. Or one of these elements might be ascendant or missing altogether. It is the ambiguous outcome, generally part of political action, that creates divisions of opinion and differences of assessment. This at least is an uncontested principle of political life. How the various decision makers confront these sets of circumstances, using the familiar triad of interest, power, and morality, defines the political drama.

One discomfort with realism among both friends and foes is that it is not grandly predictive and given to sweeping promises. Following the human nature paradigm, there is a certain cyclical and repetitive outcome to political operations and no issue is likely to be finally decided. It is a continuous process, often without a clear beginning and end. Nonetheless, realism does not rule out that something normatively better cannot happen if the conditions of interna-

---

43. See Kenneth W. Thompson, *Community, Diversity, and the New World Order* (Lanham, Md.: University Press of America, 1994), 269.

tional life change, making cooperation more satisfactory than confrontation, for example; but this will not lead to political perfection. This provides the critical foundation for realist international relations theory. Some have denounced realism because it allegedly did not foresee the collapse of the Soviet Union. On the contrary, the realist position is exactly what the Russian leadership (and that of the United States) followed in adopting new understandings of what was required to face its new internal and external balance of power.[44]

The core idea of realism, not necessarily as grand as an all-encompassing theory, will be traced from its historical and philosophical origins to demonstrate this thread of continuity in mankind's search for security, and how this project shapes the face of the realities of the present and what one can reasonably anticipate in the future. American foreign policy is inevitably involved in the outcome at the same time that it establishes new normative goals that may create a larger world community of interests.

44. For a contrary view, see Richard Ned Lebow and Thomas Resse-Kappen, *International Relations Theory and the End of the Cold War* (New York: Columbia University Press, 1995). Also, on the failure of international relations theory as exhibited by not predicting the end of the Cold War, see Peter J. Katzenstein, "Alternate Perceptions on National Security," *Items, Social Science Research Council* 49 (1995): 89–93.

1   The Legacy of the Peloponnesian War: Lessons from History

If we want to accept the realist reliance on the perduring character of human nature, at least as a hypothesis, then we need to test and verify this thesis insofar as possible. An impressive list of happenings and statements in support of this characteristic has already been given in the Introduction. There will be exceptions, to be sure, but such is the nonscientific nature of this subject matter. We will continue the search for collaborative material, however, and the first place to look is history itself, to see what additional evidence can be found to reinforce the claim that within certain limits (and with occasional variations or even at times countercases), political leaders act from a combination of self-interest, a lust for power, and a concern for morality. These characteristics generally explain the way mankind performs in the political arena. It is an error, I believe, to try to assert for human nature a completely scientific character, comparable to that of the natural and physical sciences. This would ordinarily not need to be mentioned, except that the efforts to make "social science" actually scientific—always the same formula and always a predictive result—persist in some quarters, such as in positivism, rational choice theory, and democratic development theory. This is not true of all the practitioners but enough to warrant a protest against this kind of "social science." The right interpretation of this issue was expressed by Hans J. Morgenthau, for example, when he clearly outlined the limits of social science compared to the natural sciences.[1] This reasonable stance, long argued by the opponents of the Enlightenment insofar as its claims for social science and the perfectibility of man are concerned, did not hamper Karl Marx in the last century. He insisted that economics provides an unerring guide to the whole social and political development of society; nor does it interfere with the extreme claims of rational choice proponents as they

1. See Chap. 5 of Morgenthau, *Scientific Man vs. Power Politics*, 122–52.

project the idea of economic maximization of the marketplace into political science, sociology, and so on, both to explain and to predict events of the future.

The realist claim for the value of studying human nature is much more modest; it holds that the triad of interest, power, and morality sets a rough parameter of how people are likely to make political decisions. Variations come from the relative weight of each element of this mix, interpretations and conjectures if you will, which are of value in avoiding the excesses of imagination and utopianism when faced with concrete problems. Therefore, when social scientists proclaim formulas of true scientific gravity, one must promptly part company. Politics simply does not operate with the precision of physics. There is some danger in a contrary position. In the most ambitious of the "third wave" promoters of the inevitability of the development of democracy around the world following the collapse of communism, there is still a kind of celebratory mode. Yet some of the leaders of this discipline, like Samuel P. Huntington, are well aware of the contingencies and the role of human nature in moderating the acceleration of democratic trends, through the engine of intellectual pluralism and the free market, at all times and in all places.[2] Democracies formed since the 1970s all over the globe claim to be in a period of "consolidation" of their democratic characteristics and institutions. The extreme members of the third wave school can analyze the objective situation in democracies everywhere— from the fragile new systems in Eastern Europe to the robust examples of Taiwan and South Korea in Asia. They speak with confidence of future, forward-looking democratic trends. They acknowledge the possibility of the Dulles era "rollback" or the more popular example of the "red return," when recycled former communists appear on the scene as allegedly new authentic democrats. All in all, there is a reluctance to accept the possibility of systems failure among the putative new democracies, and there are many new categories to cover the aberrations from a straightforward democratic outcome. But such an enterprise is altogether legitimate just as it is in some quarters probably altogether feckless. The ideology of democracy, at the conclusion of the Cold War, is everywhere; the reality, if language means anything, is something else altogether.

In addition to the rich lode of history, we can also in modern times turn to the field of psychology, which tries to explain ourselves to ourselves. According to the presuppositions of realism, several twentieth-century psychologists are of particular value, including Freud, Adler, and Jung. They support the historiography of realism analysis by explaining the motivation of the individual as self-

---

2. See Samuel P. Huntington, *The Third Wave: Democratization in the Late Twentieth Century* (Norman: University of Oklahoma Press, 1991).

interest and power. Insofar as this analysis is self-oriented, it is not supportive of the morality feature, except in critical moments of choice, in determining individuals' interests. Rational choice as well concentrates first on the individual as actor and not on the more complicated level of group decisions where morality, in a thin sense, comes into play. Adler and Jung, for example, see the individual possessed by his or her own interests and pleasures as permanent aspects of the human character. As we shall see later, especially in our examination of the thought of the Abbé de Saint Pierre, there are variations on what motivates people; yet, for me, there is certainly enough consensus of the dominance of self-interest and power to explain man as a political animal (although Machiavelli as discussed in Chapter 2 may carry this idea too far). That men in their ego and passion misunderstand and miscalculate these interests is not only possible but documented (Hitler, Hirohito, and Gorbachev, for example, in modern history). But choose they must; in the end, man is the moral residue of his choices.[3]

Donald Kagan's book *On the Origins of War and the Preservation of Peace* (ranging from 431 to 404 B.C. through the Cold War) provides insight about the human condition in regard to both why wars begin and why peace is more an aberration than war. "A persistent and repeated error through the ages has been the failure to understand that the preservation of peace requires active effort, planning, the expenditure of resources, and sacrifices, just as war does." Further, for those expecting fundamental changes in human nature and the disappearance of war, a critical paragraph in Kagan's conclusion is the following:

> Our study of the episodes examined here suggests some general observations about the origins of war and the preservation of peace. The first is that in a world of sovereign states contests among them over the distribution of power is the normal condition and that such contests often lead to war. Another observation is that the reasons for seeking power are often not merely the search for security or material advantage. Among them are demands for greater prestige, respect, deference, in short, honor. Since such demands involve judgments even more subjective than those about material advantage, they are still harder to satisfy. Other reasons emerge from fear, often unclear and intangible, not always of immediate threats, but also of more distant ones, against which reassurance may not be possible. The persistence of such thinking in a wide variety of states and systems over the space of millennia suggests the unwelcome conclusion that war is probably part of the human condition and likely to be with us for some time yet.[4]

3. Also see Wight, *International Theory*, Chap. 2.
4. Kagan, *On the Origins of War*, 569.

If Kagan's analysis is correct, it is difficult to accept the argument that democracies do not ever go to war with each other.

The persistence of power and interest and the difficulty of morality in asserting itself are summarized in an equally pessimistic statement: "Statistically, war has been more common than peace, and extended periods of peace have been rare in a world divided into multiple states. The cases we have examined indicate that a good will, unilateral disarmament, the avoidance of alliances, teaching and preaching the evils of war by those states who, generally satisfied with the state of the world, seek to preserve peace, are of no avail."[5]

Yet for all this wisdom, based on the evidence presented in the book, Kagan is willing to hope for, if not expect, important changes in the moral sentiments of today's mankind that would have been inconceivable to the humanity that lived in the Greek and Roman worlds. Here he cites, most importantly, the message of the Sermon on the Mount and the contrast between the old "warrior" societies and modern America, for example: "The martial values and the respect for power have not entirely disappeared, but they have been overlaid by other ideas and values, some of them unknown to the classical republics."[6] Here he drifts down Wight's rationality trail, one of Wight's three categories of international relations (rational, realist, and revolutionary).

As we undertake our search for confirmation, finding the early roots of philosophy concerned with international relations is relatively easy. Historical accident, the preservation of some written records and not others, leads us quickly to Thucydides (about 450–400 B.C.), one of the earliest historians of note, and his account of the Peloponnesian War. The war lasted from 431 B.C. to 404 B.C., although marked by various truces during the twenty-seven-year period. Thucydides failed to complete the history of the final few years, which was left to Xenophon in his *Hellenica*. The great themes, however, of this epic battle between Athens, the sea power, and Sparta and its allies of the Peloponnesian peninsula, the land power, raised in the eyes of some observers during the Cold War an uncertain parallel between the Soviet Union and its allies, on the one hand, and the United States and the rest of the West on the other. The lessons of both wars are complex and could be used in a variety of ways. Our interest will largely center on the insight we may obtain from the Greek world as to how the political leaders of that era were motivated and what relevance that may have to the present situation.

How did such a devastating war come about? Some of the background is pro-

5. Ibid., 570.
6. Ibid., 571.

vided by Plutarch (A.D. 45 to A.D. 120) in his "lives" reports, particularly the one on Pericles, the premier Greek leader at the critical prelude to the war. He adds to Thucydides' appreciation by reporting a particular incident. As the Spartans were growing uneasy about their erstwhile Athenian allies from the campaign against Persia (abetted by the envy toward Athens and continuing plots and conspiracies, which were the order of the day), Pericles proposed that all Greeks, wherever they resided, be invited to send delegates to Athens. Their purpose would be a celebration of the recent Greek victory over the Persians, a renewal of vows to the gods, and a pledge to security and freedom of the seas. (Athens was dependent on imported food and especially timber for ship construction.) Sparta looked upon this, not unreasonably, as an operation by Athens to claim hegemony throughout Greece. Sparta therefore secretly opposed and sabotaged such a gathering. Plutarch adds: "I have mentioned this episode, however, as an illustration of Pericles' lofty spirit and of the grandeur of his conceptions."[7] Nonetheless, Pericles' statecraft was essentially defensive, strengthening Athens' hold on the possessions it already had and restricting its efforts to Greece proper, a principle that was later abandoned, in the disastrous campaign against Sicily. In the early negotiations, Pericles revealed himself as a thorough, cautious leader. He did not wish to have a war with Sparta. He had a large network of agents in Sparta who regularly received his largesse, if not to prevent war, at least to delay it.[8]

The opening pages of Book I set the scene for this epic encounter. Thucydides himself had been an Athenian general in the early years of the war; a military setback resulted in his dismissal and exile. Like other officials in other ages and climes, he decided to change his profession and become a writer or, in effect, a war correspondent with particular credentials for this enterprise. So his story begins. "Thucydides, an Athenian, wrote the history of the war in which the Peloponnesians [Spartans] and the Athenians fought against one another. He began to write when they first took up arms, believing that it would be great and memorable above any previous war. For he argued that both states were then at the full height of their military power, and he saw the rest of the Hellenes either siding or intending to side with one or the other of them. No moment ever stirred Hellas more deeply than this; it was shared by many of the Barbarians and might be said even to affect the world at large."[9] Certainly it af-

7. See Plutarch, *The Rise and Fall of Athens: Nine Greek Lives* (London: Penguin, 1960), 184–85.

8. See also Thucydides, *On Justice, Power and Human Nature: The Essence of Thucydides' History of the Peloponnesian War*, ed. and trans. Paul Woodruff (Indianapolis: Hackett, 1993).

9. Benjamin Jowett, trans., *Thucydides*, 2d ed. (Oxford: Clarendon Press, 1900), Vol. 1, Book 1, p. 1.

fected the operating world, so to speak: the islands of the Aegean Sea; Asia Minor and the Persians; and the Greek relations with their colonies and the barbarians in Sicily and Italy. It does not take much imagination to see the fleets of triremes with their sails set and oars flashing, pursuing this bloody and possibly unnecessary war, save for self-interest, power, and morality—or, as Thucydides put it, they went to war out of "fear, interest, and honor." All of these guideposts are little more than that; for it is the rendering of these generalities into the decisions of the hour that sets the course and makes the history understandable, refracted through the human personalities of that time.

Thucydides paints his canvas for the war, analyzing how the earlier society was formed, the prevalence of piracy, and the rise of kings made rich by their wars in the East, against Persia. Agamemnon was able to form expeditions to Troy for loot because other princes would follow him "not from good-will, but from fear." The expedition to Troy was not large, not because of the lack of more men and ships, but because of the difficulty of providing provisions. Poverty was the real reason why the achievements of former ages were insignificant. A clear picture of the historical developments in those times is difficult to obtain because of the lack of precise information and a habit that Thucydides noted: "So little trouble do men take in the search after truth; so readily do they accept whatever comes first to hand." Thucydides does relate with confidence the earlier battle of Marathon, between Athens and the Persians, and then an even larger Persian attack that temporarily united Athens and Sparta; once victorious, the two rivals and their allies intermittently fought and negotiated a peace. This was the general situation on the peninsula that prevailed before the slow development of a crisis that led to the war. The cause of the war is a familiar paradigm for those who are influenced by the realist tradition. "The real though unavowed cause I believe to have been the growth of Athenian power, which terrified the Lacedaemonians [Spartans] and forced them into war."[10]

In today's terms, the Spartans saw the balance of power moving in the Athenians' direction. This had come about not really through the Athenians' doing but was precipitated by the meddling of the Corinthians against the Corcyreans. The Corcyreans feared they would be attacked and believed that the best way to avoid this was an alliance with Athens. Other considerations aside, this posed problems for the Athenians because of a treaty with Sparta guaranteeing the peace. As was the custom, the Corcyreans sent an embassy to Athens to pursue this aim; and then the Corinthians, learning of this maneuver, also sent an embassy to Athens to argue their case. The long exposition of the

10. Ibid., 7, 15, 17.

Corcyreans came to this: "To sum up as shortly as possible, embracing both general and particular considerations, let this show you the folly of sacrificing us. Remember that there are but three considerable naval powers in Hellas, Athens, Corcyra, and Corinth, and that if you allow two of these three to become one, and Corinth to secure us for herself, you will have to hold the sea against the united fleets of Corcyra and Peloponnese. But if you receive us, you will have our ships to reinforce you in the struggle." The Corinthian emissaries argued, however, that every power had the right to punish its own (former) allies and that the Athenians should not join forces with the Corcyreans and violate the treaty with Peloponnese: "This is that very crisis in which he who lends aid is most a friend, and he who opposes is most a foe. And for these Corcyreans—neither receive them into alliance in our dispute, nor be their abettors in crime. So do, and you will act as we have a right to expect of you, and at the same time best consult your own interest."[11]

The Athenians, recognizing the threat to their own security, at first were inclined to leave the matter alone and accept the arguments of the Corinthians. Finally, through the influence of Pericles, they agreed to a compromise, to help the Corcyreans in a defensive way, a halfway strategy that, according to Kagan, led to war, which a more resolute strategy might have avoided.[12] Still, the war was not yet in the fire, so to speak, and it remained to Sparta's allies to convince her of Athens' ambitions, which were largely undefined at that moment. Pericles was still cautious and defensive-minded and unconvinced of the wisdom of an extensive war. Once again the Corinthians were the most adamant in their efforts to rouse Spartan sensibilities as well as those of their allies: "The confidence which you feel in your constitution and social order, inclines you to receive any reflections of ours on other powers with a certain skepticism. Hence springs your moderation, but hence also the rather limited knowledge which you betray in dealing with foreign politics. . . . The Athenians are addicted to innovation, and their designs are characterized by swiftness alike in conception and execution; you have a genius for keeping what you have got, accompanied by a total want of invention, and when forced to act you never go far enough. Again, they are adventurous beyond their power, and daring beyond their judgment, and in danger they are sanguine; your wont is sanctioned by your judgment, and to fancy that from danger there is no release."[13] And so on, a speech

---

11. Ibid., 19.

12. Kagan, *On the Origins of War*, 73–74.

13. Thucydides, *The History of the Peloponnesian War* (London: J. M. Dent, 1993), Everyman's Library, Book I, 33.

that pricked the Spartans' conscience and prepared them for war. Upon hearing this news, Pericles, a friend of the Spartan king (there was but one, not the usual two at the moment), tried to stave off the war, but a series of these small steps, taken one by one, resulted in this historic conflict.

Thrusts and parries of the Athenians and their allies against the Peloponnesian alliance finally ended the peace in 431 B.C. Athens was defeated in 404 B.C. but was restored, albeit not to its former glory. While the rich story of the Peloponnesian War and its heroes and antiheroes is a historical treasure in its own right, from the perspective of ethics and statecraft, from our three pillars of realism, there is one particular incident that earns our attention: the Melian dialogue. Some accuse Thucydides of being pro-Spartan (and after being cashiered, there were grounds for his disaffection) for covering this minor story in such detail considering the length of time and the scope of the war. It makes the Athenians look bad, although often in such otherwise stark incidents there are attenuating details not without interest. Some present it as evidence of a lack of ethics in politics, a pre-Machiavellian deed without conscience; others claim that it represents the ultimate victory of truth speaking to power. It is worth our close attention also in considering the question of the malleability of human nature over the millennia.

This incident occurred in the sixteenth year of the war, as the two sides jockeyed for position at what proved to be the end of a six-year lull in the fighting. Pericles was long dead (429 B.C.) and other leaders such as Nicias and Alcibiades had come to the fore. In the summer of the sixteenth year (415 B.C.) the Athenians landed a substantial force on the small island of Melos, about halfway between Cyprus to the south and Athens. Melos was a colony of the Spartans but had tried to maintain a neutral pose during the war. In preparation for the renewal of hostilities, the Athenians were repairing their alliances and sought to enlist the Melians on their side. The Athenian envoys were received by the Melian magistrates, who preferred to do the negotiating without the inclusion of the people at large. Presumably they had some reason to fear that their position might be different from that of the rank and file. The Athenians picked up on this possibility, saying that since they were not being allowed to speak to the people, the Melian few should simply pose questions to the Athenian statements rather than go through the usual speeches. The Melians, noting the Athenian military force, responded that "you are come to be judges in your own cause, and that all we can reasonably expect from this negotiation is war, if we prove to have right on our side and refuse to submit, and in the contrary case, slavery." Before leaving for Melos, the Athenians had been instructed by the assembly to be firm with the Melians and keep the bargaining direct and to the point. The Athenian reply therefore was unambiguous: "You know as well as we do that right, as the world goes, is only a question between equals in power, while the strong do what they can and the weak suffer what they must."[14] The Jowett translation words it this way: "We both alike know that into the discussion of human affairs the question of justice only enters where there is equal power to enforce it, and that the powerful exact what they can, and the weak grant what they must."[15]

The Melians tried to change this line of talk of might to what they considered right: "We speak as we are obliged, once you enjoin us to let right alone and talk only of interest—that you should not destroy what is our common protection, the privilege of being allowed in danger to invoke what is fair and right, and even to profit by arguments not strictly valid if they can be made to persuade. And you are as much interested in this as any, as your fall would be a signal for the heaviest vengeance and an example for the world to meditate upon."[16]

The Melians next turned to the supernatural, claiming that the gods favored them; further, since they were a Spartan colony, the ties of blood would gain them support (although neutrality was their claim for safety). The Athenians responded that the gods would probably support each side equally, and that Spartan intervention on behalf of the Melians was unlikely. "Then you do not adopt the view that expediency goes with security, while justice and honour cannot be followed without danger; and danger the [Spartans] generally court as little as possible." As for the nature of men, "Of the gods we believe, and of men we know, that by a necessary law of their nature, they rule whenever they can. And it is not as if we were the first to make this law, or to act upon it when made: we found it existing before us, and shall leave it to exist forever after us; all we do is to make use of it, knowing that you and everybody else, having the same power as we have, would do the same as we do."[17]

The Athenians continued to point up the fact that the Melians were inferior in regard to power and argued that they should not consider it disgraceful to capitulate to the demand that they join the Athenians as an ally. But the Melians persisted. "We will not in a moment surrender that liberty which our city, founded seven hundred years ago, still enjoys; we will trust to the good fortune which, by the favor of the gods, has hitherto preserved us, and for human help

---

14. Ibid., 289.
15. Jowett, trans., *Thucydides*, Vol. 2, Book 5, p. 169.
16. Ibid., 290.
17. Ibid., 292.

to the [Spartans], and endeavor to save ourselves. We are ready however to be your friends, and the enemies neither of you nor the [Spartans], and we ask you to leave our country when you have made such a peace as may appear to be in the interest of both parties."[18]

The Athenians predicted the complete failure of the Melian plan and the complete ruin of Melos. The Athenians invested the city, suffering minor incursions from the Melians, pinpricks that provoked the Athenians to send reinforcements during the winter of the seventeenth year, which resulted in the Melian surrender. "The Athenians thereupon put to death all who were of military age, and made slaves of the women and children. They then colonized the island, sending thither five hundred settlers of their own."[19]

There is much of relevance to discuss here; this account from antiquity has a modern ring, despite the obvious differences in the cultural situation then and now. The cruelty of the disposition of the captives seems excessive, although the treatment of the civilian population and prisoners in the former Yugoslavia in the 1990s seems to be on a par, demonstrating, contrary to our preferences, the persistence of human behavior under similar circumstances now as then. Further, more needs to be said about the outcome, that is, the lesson of this interchange. The obvious lesson was not the final answer. The Athenian insistence on simply telling the Melians what was in store for them and warning them to become allies or face certain destruction was self-defeating. Such an approach might best be described not as realism but as European realpolitik of the seventeenth through mid-nineteenth centuries, when the raison d'état was enough justification for the decision of the king. Yet here too, when we consider both Machiavelli and Kant, we will discover more nuanced reasons, even obligations and duties, that are not always apparent on the surface, as well as superficial explanations for complex behavior.

A more interesting dimension of the dialogue is how correct the Melian position was in lecturing the Athenians on how they must behave to inferiors in strength if they were to win the war. The Athenians had always treated their allies and colonies firmly, demanding taxes and various levies, and saw to it that their naval forces, for example, posed no threat to Athens. In brief, its democratic constitution and form of government did not apply to others. Sparta, by contrast, with its authoritarian tradition and monarchical constitution, treated its allies and colonies much better, partly because Helots (slaves) outnumbered free men by a ratio of five to one and revolt was not only possible but did occur

18. Ibid., 294.
19. Ibid., 177.

from time to time, even, for example, during the course of the Peloponnesian War itself. So the Melians put their finger on a sore point during the dialogue when they forewarned the Athenians of the possible defeat of their empire if they did not treat their allies better, or, in the case of Melos, if they did not prefer their neutrality to their enmity. To this the Athenians replied that lenient treatment of Melos would be interpreted by Athens' enemies as lack of courage, presumably bringing about similar problems with allies, but out of disrespect rather than fear.

One element in realist thought is the need to respect the legitimate views and concerns of potential friends and enemies alike and to be willing to yield on matters that are not central to one's interests. According to Morgenthau, "Diplomacy must look at the political scene from the point of view of other nations."[20] The violation of this simple and sensible principle by the Athenians was an error of statesmanship that they paid for dearly in their ultimate defeat by Sparta and its allies. Rather than looking upon the Melian dialogue as the essence of smart and tough politics, one should view it as a prize historical example of blind power overreach, inimical to the real interest of Athens and contrary to the spirit of moral choice and good sense that often motivated Athenian conduct. Plutarch's eulogy of Pericles, for example, gives a sense of the realist perspective. As reported by Plutarch, the plague took a heavy toll on Athens when workers in the fields came into the walled area, destroying Pericles' friends and family and finally claiming Pericles himself.

> Pericles deserves our admiration, then, not only for the sense of justice and the serene temper that he preserved amidst the many crises and intense personal hatreds which surrounded him, but also for his greatness of spirit. He considered it the highest of all his claims to honour that, despite the immense power he wielded, he had never given way to feelings of envy or hatred and had treated no man as so irreconcilable an enemy that he could never become his friend. This fact, by itself, it seems to me, removes any objection to his otherwise pretentious and childish nickname (the "Head," because of his large, long head) and, indeed, gives it a certain aptness: a character so gracious and a life so pure and uncorrupt in the exercise of sovereign power might well be called Olympian, according to our conception of the race of gods who rule over the universe as the authors of all good things and as beings who are by nature incapable of evil.[21]

This is a most generous tribute and ignores a good deal of Pericles' political, military, and personal career that Plutarch himself reports, sometimes unflat-

20. See Morgenthau, *Politics among Nations*, 3d ed., 563.
21. Ibid., 205.

teringly, in the same chronicle. This places Pericles almost alone as a Wightian revolutionary in a nation of realists.

We will now move in time and place from Athens to Rome and Florence at the end of the fifteenth century to look at a new development in international relations, as practiced at a fairly low level and recommended to power at a very high level indeed. We will consider Machiavelli primarily in *The Prince* but also in *The Discourses.*

2   Machiavelli: History and Human Nature

The fascination over the ages with the writings of Niccolò Machiavelli (1469–1527) may be in part because of the richness of the interpretation of his works; the authors of the thousands of books about him and his philosophy are all certain that they have authentic insight into the subject. As recently as 1989 a new interpretation, by Sebastian de Grazia, won the Pulitzer Prize for biography.[1] Opponents and supporters of the Florentine philosopher have proven to be a remarkably literary lot.

There have been extravagant claims about the importance of his writing, especially in his brief and powerful *The Prince*, asserting that it opened a new horizon in politics, separating politics from morality. Was Machiavelli's theory original, or did he simply have the courage to put down in writing what his contemporaries in power, in higher offices than he was able to achieve, were saying? Or does that particular insight require more consideration? *The Prince* and *The Discourses on Livy* were written concurrently, the former from the (autobiographical) viewpoint of a cunning court official and the latter representing Machiavelli in the more prudent but passionate role of a republican Italian nationalist.[2]

This point alone is enough to help us understand that here is no simple philosopher of power but a man of complexity, purpose, and passion. There is no question that he was (retrospectively) a pivotal figure toward the end of the medieval era, marking the transition from the old to the new, on the cusp of the Renaissance and the preparation for the Enlightenment that have attracted so much scholarship to his historical career. His works were first translated into

---

1. Sebastian de Grazia, *Machiavelli in Hell* (Princeton: Princeton University Press, 1989).

2. Niccolò Machiavelli, *The Prince* (London: Penguin, 1995), and *Discourses on Livy* (London: Penguin, 1983).

English in 1640, and by 1700 his name was considered synonymous with that of the devil. Thomas Macaulay said, "We doubt whether any in literary history be so generally odious as that of the man whose character and writings we now propose to consider."[3] It is not necessary for us to enter into those aspects of his legacy, but rather to concentrate on those parts of his method and philosophy that are relevant to our consideration of his relationship to ethics and statecraft.

Machiavelli was born in Florence, Italy, in 1469 and died there in 1527. His father was a lawyer, and his family background can be described as middle class. In 1498 he was appointed secretary and second chancellor to the Florentine Republic, which gave him entry to a certain level of diplomacy of the day. He traveled regularly by horse and coach to France and Spain but particularly to the Papal States. He knew the courts of Louis XII and the emperor Maximilian; he was with Caesar Borgia in the Romagne, part of the Papal States; and after the papal elections of 1503, he accompanied Pope Julius II on his first campaign of conquest. In 1507, as chancellor of the newly established Florentine militia (a favorite project of his, as part of his aversion to foreign mercenaries), he organized an infantry force that fought at the capture of Pisa in 1509. Three years later this force was defeated as the French, Spanish, and papal forces brought the Medici family back to power in Florence. This development, despite his best efforts, effectively ended Machiavelli's diplomatic career. He was dismissed and accused of plotting against the Medici; he was imprisoned and tortured but then released to retire (unwillingly) to his modest farm, barely within sight of the buildings of his beloved city. He had the leisure, then, to reflect on power and politics, what he had learned and what he might do to enter the game once again. He plunged into the writing of *The Prince* and *The Discourses on Livy*, completing them in 1513 and 1514, the first as a job application, in effect, and the second as a major historical document. Later writings included popular plays, and in 1520 he was commissioned by Cardinal Medici to write a history of Florence, which he completed in 1525. He died two years later.

Machiavelli lived in an era of great political turmoil in his native city of Florence. Italy was experiencing parlous times of division and strife, with the country divided into five primary power areas, none of which had the strength to unify Italy and restore her to her past glories. Foreign invasion since 1494, when King Charles of France invaded Naples, had taken its toll, and then with Louis XII the situation worsened because the Spanish also became involved in Italian wars and politics. Machiavelli, an ardent Florentine patriot and also an Italian nationalist (these terms were not synonymous), served his own city well for

3. Quoted in Machiavelli, *The Prince*, ix.

fourteen years, and his writings aimed at preserving those dual interests, even if they were only partially appreciated.

What was the principal lesson Machiavelli had learned during his diplomatic career that should be brought to the attention of the new Medici rulers? Perhaps he could save them from blunders, the historical blunders that had been the object of his reflection, so that they would be secure in office. If he brought this wisdom and practical experience to their attention, perhaps they would reward him with office. It was in this high mode of expectation that he sent his thin book with an accompanying letter to "The Magnificent Lorenzo de Medici." Gold and riches Machiavelli had none to offer, but among his belongings, he has not "found anything . . . so dear or that I value as much as my understanding of the deeds of great men, won by me from a long acquaintance with contemporary affairs and a continuous study of the ancient world, these matters I have very diligently analyzed and pondered for a long time, and now, having summarized them in a little book, I am sending them to Your Magnificence."[4]

The summary was a practical treatise on government, the various types of government then in vogue, and how to seize and keep power. That was the supreme moral end of the enterprise. Every other consideration was secondary, and the prince who did not keep his eye on that goal was certain to lose his principality to those who played the game according to Machiavelli's rules. The same was true for the sovereign of a republic. In *The Prince* it was naturally the principality that Machiavelli focused on, although in *The Discourses*, his republican preferences were obvious. There is, however, nothing incompatible in the two books, simply differences of emphasis depending on the target audience.[5]

From the standpoint of looking for corroboration of my thesis that there is a historical continuity of human nature, a certain immutability of actions people are likely to take in similar (but not identical) circumstances, Machiavelli is a good confirming source. He would have been perfectly at home in the world of Hans J. Morgenthau, and vice versa. Herbert Butterfield helps us in our task in his book *The Statecraft of Machiavelli*. One section of this book deals with Machiavelli's historiography, the inductive method, focusing on example and imitation. According to Butterfield, "The theories in question were first of all a doctrine of 'imitation'; this conditioned Machiavelli's attitude to the great men of the past; secondly, an important thesis concerning historical recurrence, one that affected therefore the problem of the deduction of general laws from his-

---

4. Ibid., 29.

5. For a discussion of this point, see the introduction to Machiavelli, *Discourses*.

torical data, and thirdly, a conviction of the superiority of the ancient world as a guide to human behavior in the present."[6] Machiavelli's first principle therefore was the great historical example.

The second, Butterfield writes, "was based on the view that human nature is unchanged throughout the ages."[7] Beyond that, Machiavelli was convinced, based on his historical examples, that the bold stroke could always make an important difference. He was also acutely aware of the price of choice (a moral element that he did not acknowledge but which was nonetheless before him as much as it was Reinhold Niebuhr): "So men are free to choose—men with virtue at least. But they must know their choice. And sometimes the price of achieving one set of values is, in terms of another set of values, almost unbearable."[8] Also, in our consideration of Machiavelli and morality and virtue, we must keep in mind the conflict for him between two moralities, Christian and pagan. In regard to means and ends, Machiavelli was no follower of Augustine or Aquinas. A good end for Machiavelli justified the evil means. This places him in opposition to Immanuel Kant as well.

J. H. Whitfield has additional insight into both Machiavelli and his times: "Machiavelli admires, when and where he finds it, the force and energy of mind that knows and does. His hero is the tamer of man and nature, 'the one who understands and rules natural and human forces, and makes them his instrument.' " The era absorbed the attention of many writers and philosophers, and that combination of events, plus the personality of Machiavelli, fortunately left to us in books and letters, accounts in part for the volume of literature. We turn to Whitfield again: "It is my business here to examine the culture of the Renascence at the point where it becomes painfully aware of politics. The point is Machiavelli's. For he does not represent . . . the double degeneracy of both politics and culture. He represents instead the culture that is born of humanism becoming aware of political problems because they are at a crisis. It is because of this that he seeks to solve them from the element which has endorsed the western mind. But for those reasons, we are obliged to examine the crisis which precipitates his writing."[9] And this we have already covered, namely, the end of the Florentine Republic and the return of the Medici.

Whitfield then returns to the moral question: "Unless *The Prince* is read as the specific remedy to an otherwise insoluble problem it is divorced from the

---

6. Herbert Butterfield, *The Statecraft of Machiavelli* (New York: Collier Books, 1960), 24.

7. Ibid., 26.

8. Machiavelli, *Discourses*, 61.

9. J. H. Whitfield, *Machiavelli* (Oxford: Basil Blackwell, 1947), 18.

content and its sense." He continues, "For Machiavelli to mean well is insufficient to the task of doing good; he establishes a different but an equally logical, and an equally moral, criterion. If the intention is inadequate to its scope, then it has elements of badness. One cannot destroy the world and take no blame for it."[10]

Machiavelli's importance in the history of politics and power, as is routinely noted, is his deliberate separation of morality from politics. He emphasized that when the safety of the country was at stake, questions of justice or injustice did not apply. Whether this stance is such a departure from common sense and practice as some political scientists of a later era insist is something to ponder as we review Machiavelli as he relates to our subject. His writings propose that the prince can and should resort to any stratagem to preserve his hold on a particular state. These possibilities include awarding the necessary bureaucracy with honors and financial emoluments—or eliminating them altogether in a relatively small blood purge. These actions would equally assure the continuity of the state. Yet the often overlooked morality of this line of argument is the assumption that the state is the primary moral value that must be protected and preserved at all costs. This is a very modern argument, and to say that Machiavelli was uninterested in the moral argument is to skew his approach to the key problem of statecraft, as it was understood in his age as well as ours. The relevant part of Machiavelli's argument for the conduct of policy in international (as well as domestic) affairs comes down to three main considerations, two of which I have discussed in part.

The first consideration is the question of historiography, which we relied on Herbert Butterfield to explain. Machiavelli reviewed, as it was available to him, how leaders great and not so great behaved during recorded history. The second is the question of human nature and whether it is malleable or unchanging; and the third, whether these two insights justify the claim for a break with the past and the creation of a new "social science" or whether they simply reinforce our subsequent ideas of the relationship between politics and idealistic aspirations.

In regard to history, Machiavelli was one with the scholarship of the time, looking upon the history of mankind as he knew it as a cyclical phenomenon. This view was inherited from the Greeks and held Europe in its sway until the Enlightenment, when the idea of linear progress rose to ascendancy. But in Machiavelli's time, the Golden Age was in the past, as everyone knew, and the Bronze and Iron Ages were infinitely inferior. Evidence was at hand in the re-

10. Ibid., 63, 72.

cordings of the heroic deeds of the past, not to mention the glory of Rome, that the present was worse than the past and that the future, in all likelihood, would be worse than the present. History, then, was a storehouse of knowledge waiting to be recovered and adapted to the present. The best guide for the present was to be mindful of the past and to follow good examples. One could do no better than to be imitative.

An important aspect of Machiavelli's approach, therefore, was the search for the right examples. Some have described this as a "scientific approach" (Butterfield) and hail Machiavelli's work as the precursor of modern political science, or even the social sciences (a heavy burden indeed). This was a prescientific age, and crediting or blaming Machiavelli for this method of approach seems to stretch the facts, although the interpretation does exist in the literature. We are not, however, entering into the aspects of the argument over the legacy of Machiavelli in that sense. His historical approach, the axial concern between antiquity and his time, and the careful concentration on inductive or specific examples, distinguishes him from previous Western writers on politics. He also had a specific task at hand, trying to ingratiate himself with the new rulers. Here is his statement of how useful his advice might well be. A new principality requires special attention and poses more hazards than a long-established principality for a new royal ruler:

> First, if it is not completely new but a new appendage to an old state (so that the territory as a whole can be called composite) disorders arise chiefly because of one natural difficulty always encountered in new principalities. What happens is that men willingly change their ruler, expecting to fare better. This expectation induces them to take up arms against him; but they only deceive themselves, and they learn from experience that they have made matters worse. This follows from another common and natural necessity: a prince is always compelled to injure those who have made him the new ruler, subjecting them to the troops and imposing the endless other hardships which this new conquest entails. As a result you are opposed by all those you have injured in occupying the principality, and you cannot keep the friendship of those who have put you there; you cannot satisfy them in the way they had taken for granted, yet you cannot use strong medicine on them, for you are in their debt. For always, no matter how powerful one's armies, in order to enter a country one needs the goodwill of the inhabitants.[11]

Machiavelli then goes into his pattern of historical example, pursuing his inductive technique. He was not anticipating any historical progress; such ideas were contrary to his and his contemporaries' understanding of history. Each

---

11. Machiavelli, *The Prince*, 6.

nation went through an inexorable, cyclical progression: a descent from prosperity to adversity, followed, it was hoped, by a rise. Nations inevitably became corrupted; when this happened, the greatness of the state could be restored by a man comparable in stature to the state's original and principal founder. There was no particular ethic at work in this process; his view was highly consequentialist. What worked was what mattered.

In carrying out his policies, the prince had three factors, or principles, to take into account. First was *necessito*. This was the ultimate justification against the charges that critics of the prince might well raise. If the prince thought that a certain action was necessary to preserve his power, then *necessito* was the word of the moment. It was the ultimate moral argument, since keeping power was the highest end of government. Those who would not accept the *necessito* argument but would explain it away as mere rationalization were not living in the times of the city-states. The technology of the day made ruling dangerous. The armaments and skills of the ruler's forces were only on a par with those of his many contemporaries; the availability of mercenary forces made the balance of forces, the order of battle, so to speak, uncertain. The strength and disposition of forces might be known or not, but the intention was always well known: to seize power whenever possible. Constant vigilance was no guarantee that guile and stealth, daggers and poisons, might make vulnerable what had appeared to be a formidable defense. So *necessito* was always available to the ruler to justify whatever had to be done, in the name of the sanctity of the sovereign.

Machiavelli's second principle to weigh in considerations of political action was *fortuna*. Fortune, he reckoned, might well be up to 50 percent of the process. In a candid moment, he says that *fortuna* is so influential that he wonders whether it is really worthwhile to agonize over decisions.

Sometimes, when thinking of this, I have myself inclined to this same opinion. Nonetheless, so as not to rule out our free will, I believe that it is probably true that fortune is the arbiter of half the things we do, leaving the other half or so to be controlled by ourselves. I compare fortune to one of those violent rivers, which, when they are enraged, flood the plains, tear down trees and buildings, wash soil from one place to deposit in another. Everyone flees before them, everybody yields to their impetus, there is no possibility of resistance. Yet although such is their nature, it does not follow that when they are flowing quietly one cannot take precautions, constructing dikes and embankments so that when the river is in flood they would keep one channel so their impetus be less wild and dangerous. So it is with fortune.[12]

12. Ibid., 130.

Machiavelli's conviction that luck plays such a large part in our lives, including those of our political leaders, rules out any expectation on his part that some emerging historicism may be the answer. He remained convinced of the value of inductive reason from empirical experience and not because of the presence or absence of a grand design. To expand on this thought, we turn to another Machiavellian insight: "Yes, constraining and shaping to one's desire is no simple thing. On this subject, I conclude, therefore, that as fortune is changeable whereas men are obstinate in their ways, men prosper as long as fortune and policy are in accord, and when there is a clash they fail. I hold strong to this: that it is better to be impetuous than circumspect: because *fortuna* is a woman and if she is to be submissive it is necessary to beat and coerce her. Experience shows that she is more often subdued by men who do this than by those who act coldly. Always, being a woman, she favors young men, because they are less circumspect and more ardent, and because they command her with greater audacity."[13]

The third principle that Machiavelli recommends to the prince is *virtu*. The word creates translation difficulties, not the easy one from Italian to English, but rather the cultural translation from the political setting of medieval Italy to the present. Leo Strauss touches on this in his essay on Machiavelli in *History of Political Philosophy*.[14] According to Strauss, Machiavelli in effect edited Aristotle's *Politics* in his consideration of "virtue" as the quality present in a good person interested in leading the life of civic virtue in the Greek polis, or city-state. Such a construct, in Machiavelli's view, was not politically possible; people did not live in this ideal way. This kind of virtue was meaningless. So Machiavelli's definition of virtue was not magnanimity, but rather more a utilitarianism based on the reality of things.[15]

> It now remains for us to see how a prince must govern his conduct towards his subjects or his friends. I know that this has often been written about before, and so I hope it will not be thought presumptuous for me to do so, as, especially in discussing this subject, I draw up an original set of rules. But since my intention is to say something that will prove of practical use to the inquirer, I have thought it proper to represent things as they are in real truth, other than as they are imagined. Many have dreamed up republics and principalities which have never in truth been

---

13. Ibid., 133.

14. Leo Strauss, "Niccolò Machiavelli, 1469–1527," in *History of Political Philosophy*, ed. Leo Strauss and Joseph Cropsey, 3d ed. (Chicago: University of Chicago Press, 1987).

15. Also see Harvey C. Mansfield, *Machiavelli's Virtue* (Chicago: University of Chicago Press, 1996).

known to exist; the gulf between how one should live and how one does live is so wide that a man who neglects what is actually done for what should be done learns the way to self-destruction rather than self-preservation. The fact is that a man who wants to act virtuously in every way necessarily comes to grief among so many who are not virtuous. Therefore if a prince wants to maintain his rule he must learn how to be virtuous and to make use of this or not according to need.[16]

This observation and advice places Machiavelli in the center of the tradition of historical realism. Imaginary virtue has little appeal to a political adviser intent on preserving the power of his prince. The prince must concentrate on the world as it is, not as he or others might prefer it. This leads then to the following advice:

> So leaving aside imaginary things, and referring only to those which truly exist, I say that whenever men are discussed (and especially princes, who are more exposed to view), they are noted for various qualities which earn them either praise or condemnation. Some, for example, are held to be generous, and others miserly. . . . Some are held to be benefactors, others are called grasping; some cruel, some compassionate. . . . But because of conditions in the world, princes cannot have those qualities, or observe them completely. So a prince has of necessity to be so prudent that he knows how to escape the evil reputation attached to those vices which are not so dangerous, if he possibly can, but, if he cannot, he need not worry so much about the latter. And then, he must not flinch from being blamed for vices which are necessary for safeguarding the state. This is because, taking everything into account, he will find that some of the things that appear to be virtues will, if he practices them, ruin him, and some of the things that appear to be vices will bring him security and prosperity.[17]

The three principles of *necessito*, *fortuna*, and *virtu*, then, properly understood and practiced, were the elements for seizing, holding, and expanding power. This was essential advice for domestic policies, except that in the context of the day, one could just as readily consider them principles of interstate relations as well. The idea of necessity is expressed in the conditions of politics, social and military, and in the habits of the prince's subjects; if these conditions conspire against him, as it were, he has the object of acting against one or the other of them, usually surrounding a particular personage, and so right the situation. This tactical approach had nothing whatsoever to do with the ideas of the following centuries on how to find objective laws that would allow for the development of human society in ways that were amenable to the prince's gov-

---

16. Machiavelli, *The Prince*, 90–91.
17. Ibid., 91–92.

ernment. Machiavelli believed that the successful prince should not be afraid of getting his hands dirty in running the state or generally picking up the burden of political power.

So here we have a sketch of the classical Machiavelli, filling easily two of the key requirements of historical realism, interest and power. Yet he is not unconcerned with morality. If one equates decency with morality, there are a variety of examples in Machiavelli that may be borderline (for example, in Chapter 10, "The Constitutional Principality"). Here a private citizen becomes the ruler through the favor of his fellow citizens. He then is required to balance the interests of the people with those of the nobles and, in this competition, secure his dominion.

> A principality is created either by the people or by the nobles, according to whether the one or the other of these two classes is given the opportunity. What happens is that when the nobles see they cannot withstand the people, they start to increase the standing of one of their number, and they make him prince in order to be able to achieve their own ends under this cloak. The people in the same way, when they see they cannot withstand the nobles, increase the standing of one of themselves and make him prince in order to be protected by his authority. A man who becomes prince with the help of the nobles finds it more difficult to maintain his position than one who does so with the help of the people. As prince, he finds himself surrounded by many who believe they are his equals, and because of that he cannot command or manage them the way he wants. A man who becomes prince by favour of the people finds himself standing alone, and he has near him either no one or very few not prepared to take orders. In addition, it is impossible to satisfy the nobles favourably, without doing violence to the interests of others; but this can be done as far as the people are concerned. The people are more honest in their intentions than the nobles are because the latter want to oppress the people, whereas they only want not to be oppressed.[18]

It has often been said that study of *The Prince* and *The Discourses* will reveal that Machiavelli has a rather evenhanded view of the form of government that should prevail in fifteenth-century Italy. The principality or the republic would serve equally well, as long as it fulfilled the foremost function of government, stability. Stability was as much admired then as it is in modern times. In the study of economic and political modernization, stability is presented as the first basic requirement. This is the foundation, then, for economic development, which is by nature destabilizing but which is then reinforced by popular participation and some program of social justice. In the Florentine society, stability

18. Ibid., 30–31.

meant law and order, the reduction of violence to a tolerable condition. But as particularly the last chapter of *The Prince* reveals, Machiavelli's personal agenda was that of the Italian nationalist: he launched this plea in Chapter 26, "Exhortation to Liberate Italy from the Barbarians." This conclusion, in my view, is the ultimate concern in Machiavelli, demonstrating his moral preference, deploring the failure of the Italian princes of the day both to master the art of power and politics and to have the insight to see the moral vision of an Italy restored.

The context of Machiavelli's time assumes particular salience in the work of J. G. A. Pocock. In his book, there are two aspects of the "Machiavellian moment." The first is that the moment under consideration "is selectively and thematically defined. It is asserted that certain enduring patterns in the temporal consciousness of medieval and early modern Europe led to the presentation of the republic, and the citizen's participation in it, as constituting a problem in historical self-understanding."[19] This is certainly one plausible explanation for Machiavelli's concluding appeal for the future of Italy. This future would of course require leadership of a strong "prince," but the ultimate political strength would come from the power of the people.

The second meaning of "Machiavellian moment" in Pocock's lexicon is defining the problem. "It is a name for the moment in conceptualized time in which the republic was seen as confronting its own temporal finitude, as attempting to remain morally and politically stable in a stream of irrational events conceived as essentially destructive of all systems of secular stability."[20] From this perspective, Machiavelli and his contemporaries in politics were looking for a transition toward a republican preference that would maximize the effectiveness of the state, with due concern for interest, power, and morality.

In the meantime, in the name of Italian unity and restoration, Machiavelli appeals to the powers that are, the House of Medici, particularly since his hero, Cesare Borgia, was already dead.

> See how Italy beseeches God to send someone to save her from those barbarous cruelties and outrages; see how eager and willing the country is to follow a banner, if only someone will raise it. . . . There is the greatest readiness, and where that is so there cannot be great difficulty, provided only your House will emulate those I have singled out for admiration. As well as this, unheard of wonders are to be seen, performed by God; the sea is divided, a cloud has shown you the way, water has

---

19. J. G. A. Pocock, *The Machiavellian Moment: Florentine Political Thought and the Atlantic Republican Tradition* (Princeton: Princeton University Press, 1975), vii–viii.

20. Ibid., viii.

gushed from the rock, it has rained manna; all things have conspired to your greatness. The rest is up to you. God does not want to do everything Himself, and take
away from us our free will and our share of the glory which belongs to us.[21]

It is now clear that Machiavelli's contribution to the long, progressive path
from feudalism and a European version of a Chinese episode of warring states
was part of the process to something else, the nation-states and their monarchies gradually shifting into the republican and democratic modes of our day.
Some of the principles of deceit and deception, the rule of the Florentinian day,
have been modified in part; but the persistence of the primary features he concerned himself with, especially power, remains an important element in our
calculations of international politics today.

In our consideration of Machiavelli as a milestone in the history of political
theory—that is, a systematic criticism of the powers of the day—it is important
that we do not make him only a symbolic exemplar of Florentine politics. He
was after all a human personality, and we know a good deal about him not only
from his published writings but also from his letters to friends. One of those extant is a letter to Francesco Vettori, after Machiavelli's dismissal from office in
the Florentine Republic.

> I rise in the morning with the sun, and I go off to a wood of mine which I am hav-
> ing cut down, where I stop for two hours to see what was done the day before and
> to talk to the woodcutters who always have some trouble on hand either among
> themselves or with their neighbors. . . . Leaving the wood I go to a spring and
> thence to some bird traps of mine. I have a book with me, Dante or Petrarch or
> one of the minor poets, Tibullus, Ovid or the like. I read about their amorous pas-
> sions and their loves. I remember my own, and dwell enjoyably on those for a
> while. Then I go on to the road and into the tavern. I talk to the passers-by. I ask
> what news of their villages. I hear all sorts of things and observe the various tastes
> and ideas of men. In the meantime it is time for dinner, and with my folk, I eat
> what food this poor farm and miserable patrimony of mine provides. When I have
> eaten I go back to the tavern. Here I find the host, and usually a butcher, a miller,
> and a couple of kilnsmen. With them I degrade myself playing all day at cricca and
> tric-trac, and this gives rise to a thousand arguments and endless vexations with in-
> sulting words, and most times there is a fight over a penny, and we can be heard
> shouting from as far away as San Casciano. And so, surrounded by these lice, I
> blow the cobwebs out of my brain and relieve the unkindness of my fate, content
> that she trample on me in this way to see if she is not ashamed to treat me thus.
>   When evening comes I return home and go into my study, and at the door I

---

21. Machiavelli, *The Prince*, 135.

take off my daytime dress covered in mud and dirt, and put on royal and curial robes, and then decently attired I enter the courts of the ancients, where affectionately greeted by them, I partake of that food which is mine alone and for which I was born: where I am not ashamed to talk with them and inquire the reasons of their actions; and they out of their human kindness answer me, and for four hours at a stretch I feel no worry of any kind: I forget all my troubles. I am not afraid of poverty or death. I give myself up entirely to them. And because Dante says that understanding does not constitute knowledge unless it is retained in the memory, I have written down what I have learned from their conversation and composed a short work de Principatibus.[22]

Such were the circumstances as he wrote *The Prince* and *The Discourses*, the Hyde and Jekyll as it were of this extraordinary personality, the republican who reveled in giving advice to the prince in what became known as raison d'état but also leavened this advice with stress on the importance of keeping the support of the people.

Finally, we consider the conclusion of a work mentioned early on in this chapter, de Grazia's *Machiavelli in Hell*. As we have learned, Machiavelli's attitude toward religion was ambivalent; on balance he was a servant of God, and despite his criticism of the pope and the Papal States, at the end he asked for and was granted absolution. His often bitter quarrels with the pope were over temporal matters: why can't he increase his strength to expel the foreigners and unite Italy? True, Machiavelli also preferred the pagan virtues of courage and strength to the Christian doctrine of turning the other cheek and other tributes to weakness. In any case, according to de Grazia, when Machiavelli died, he went to hell. He discovered it was part of paradise for God's elect. Upon orientation, Machiavelli concluded that one should choose heaven for the climate but hell for the company. He also learned that on earth his friends have composed an epitaph for him.

> Niccolò Machiavelli
> For Love of country
> Pissed in many a snow.[23]

As we have now seen, from the standpoint of realism, the examples of both Thucydides and Machiavelli bolster our core argument on human nature and the significance of interest, power, and morality in the pursuit of politics. These represent the essential nature of politics, foreign and domestic; the distinction

---

22. Machiavelli, *Discourses*, 68–69.
23. Ibid., 384–85.

had not yet reached its classic proportions. By the late eighteenth century, however, these spheres had solidified, as we shall see when we consider certain aspects of the works of Immanuel Kant and his effort to go beyond human nature into institutional systems as a way of improving the outcome of international relations.

3   Kant and the Institutionalization of Peace

At about the same time Machiavelli was producing *The Prince* and *The Discourses*, telling his audience of the ubiquitous nature of evil and the wisdom of treachery, other ideas in Europe were competing vigorously for attention. Realism was holding sway in Italy, but Christianity and its handmaiden pacifism, as well as the Roman Catholic preference for the just war, were also gaining wide attention. Beginning in the sixteenth century, idealistic notions flourished around the idea of peace. Among the advocates were Erasmus, William Penn, the Abbé de Saint Pierre, Immanuel Kant, and Jeremy Bentham. Prominent interpreters and critics included Jean-Jacques Rousseau and Georg Hegel.

The cleric Erasmus in his *Adages*, published in 1527 (thirteen years after *The Prince*), inveighed against war in a book second in popularity only to the Bible. The key essay was "War Is Sweet to Those Who Have Not Experienced It": "War indeed may continue to be our lot, they admit; but we are free," said Erasmus, "to choose differently." In *The Complaint of Peace*, Erasmus questions the idea that war is inherent in human nature, or caused by unrelenting outside pressures, or by divine intervention. Animals have no such proclivity, disproving natural traits; "outside pressures" would include such things as human fraud; and of "divine intervention," said Erasmus, "this is not Christ's message but rather Satan's."[1]

Between 1514 and 1517 Erasmus devoted himself to the cause of peace, proposing a "Congress of Kings" to that end. He also wrote a manual for princes, *The Education of the Christian Prince.* His immediate target was Prince Charles

---

1. See Sissela Bok, "Early Advocates of Lasting World Peace: Utopians or Realists?" in *Ethics and International Affairs: A Reader,* ed. Joel H. Rosenthal (Washington, D.C.: Georgetown University Press), 150–67.

of Spain, who as Charles V, among other things, continued the Spanish intervention in Italy. Although Erasmus did not carry the day, nonetheless he built a
foundation so that in 1712 the Abbé de Saint Pierre proposed a permanent
league of European rulers under common laws.[2]

Immanuel Kant (1724–1804), writing in 1794 near the end of his life, brought
together many of his political philosophical ideas and applied them in an imag-
inative way in the book *Perpetual Peace.* In his *Critique of Pure Reason* and *Critique of Practical Reason,* Kant concerns himself in part with the possibility of
advancing from the state of nature, which is evil and restrictive, to the state of
morality, or practical reason. Here the individual, unlike in nature, experiences
freedom from the domination of others and begins to exercise his natural good-
ness. Historical progress reinforces these tendencies, with the imperative
(willed) goal of establishing a republican (representative) government. The
form of this government is in three parts, the legislator (as in Rousseau, the first
among equals), the executive, and the judge. The individual exercises his freedom and is protected against the government by participating in the "general
will" (another Rousseauian device). The "general will" was to provide the guarantee that sovereignty resided in the people.

The practical superiority of republicanism came to Kant in part from his observation that it was kingdoms and principalities that went to war. The real vic-
tims were always the people, not the royalty. In a world of mercenary soldiers
and the petty ambitions of princelings, so well known to Machiavelli, there was
a good deal of truth in this view. It is an idea akin to the more modern claim
that democracies do not go to war with each other. So in Kant's time, the claim
was that once monarchies were eliminated, and republics were established and
formed a gradually growing confederation, peace would be perpetual.

Kant wondered, however, about the long-term prospect of this union of republics. Should in fact these new republics form a larger organization, would
such an organization perhaps lapse into a new tyranny, negating the individual's gain of freedom in his own republic? Kant never quite decided this question. It is worthwhile, indeed, to go carefully through *Perpetual Peace* to learn
the specifics of Kant's ideas and why, in an important sense, "perpetual peace"
is the logical outcome of his life's work, the goal of his years of philosophical reflections and writings.

In a more formal way, one can offer details in Kantian philosophy as an aid
to commentary on and evaluation of Kant's requirements for perpetual peace.
This subject is considered in an introduction to the essay by R. Latta of the Uni-

2. Ibid.

versity of Glasgow in the 1903 edition of *Perpetual Peace,* reprinted in 1915 (World War I was then in full vigor). "For Kant perpetual peace is an ideal, not merely as a speculative utopian idea, with which in fancy we may play, but as a moral principle, which ought to be, and therefore, can be realized." In his philosophy, Kant makes a distinction between the mechanical, or natural, and teleological, or providential. Reason, he claims, has two aspects, theoretical and practical: "*A priori* principles of reason (e.g., substance and attribute, cause and effect . . . are valid only within the realm of possible sense-experience." Many things are outside the senses—God, the soul, the world. Sense experience is the world of nature. Ideas transcending the sense experience are established by pure practical reason, or an imperative of the world. If it ought to be, then it can be willed in a moral imperative, demanding for example, perpetual peace. Perpetual peace for Kant is a moral duty: "We must desire perpetual peace not only as a material good, but also as a state of things, resulting from new recognition of the precepts of duty." Reduced to a Kantian maxim, we have: "Seek ye first the kingdom of pure practical reason and its righteousness, and the object of your endeavor, the blessing of perpetual peace, will be added upon you."[3]

Kant begins the book by noticing a sign raised by a Dutch innkeeper, "perpetual peace," hanging above a picture of a cemetery. The idea of mankind perishing in a vast cemetery, if war is not eliminated, is a theme running through the book. Kant, a man wedded to procedures and to law as the embodiment of morality, proceeds in a formal way to establish the framework and conditions for doing away with war. His first section is titled "Containing the Preliminary Articles of Perpetual Peace between States."

First, "No treaty of peace shall be regarded as valid, if made with the secret reservation of material for a future war." He had seen this kind of bogus peace in his time in Europe. This demand is an application of Kant's categorical imperative. This idea is capable of being willed into a universal principle. Assuming universal compliance, the advance in morality would be substantial. If the signatories later conspire for war, wrote Kant, "Diplomacy of this kind only Jesuitical casuistry can justify; it is beneath the dignity of a ruler, just as acquiescence in such processes of reasoning is beneath the dignity of his minister, if one judges the facts as they really are. If, however, according to present enlightened ideas of political wisdom, the true glory of a state lies in the uninterrupted development of its power by every possible means, this judgment must cer-

3. Immanuel Kant, *Perpetual Peace: A Philosophical Essay,* 1795 (1903 ed.; reprint, New York: Macmillan, 1915), viii, ix.

tainly strike one as scholastic and pedantic."[4] The Machiavellian tradition was still a force to be reckoned with.

Point 2: "No state having an independent existence—whether it be great or small—shall be acquired by another through inheritance, purchase, or donation." Kant was against treating people as property and was also opposed to a ruler hiring mercenary troops for campaigns unrelated to the origin of the troops. The idea of the Swiss guards did not appeal to him. The citizens of a state composed a society, and in a republic they had the best opportunity to reach their full potential. "Like the trunk of a tree, it has its own roots, and to graft it on to another state is to do away with its existence as a moral person, and to make it a thing. Hence it is in contradiction to the idea of the original contract without which no right over a people is thinkable." This second principle, then, is very much in his preference to move away from kingdoms, which were prone to do exactly this with regard to other states when the opportunity arose. Republican rule would abolish such backward and "nature-oriented" practices, which blocked man's aspirations for a moral life of practical reason.[5]

Point 3: "Standing armies shall be abolished in course of time." Such armies, projecting a state of readiness for war, are a threat to others and are often among the causes of war. They are also a great financial burden on the people, costing more over a few years than a brief war. Kant did not favor hiring people to kill one another, which violated his famous categorical imperative to consider each person as an end and not a means.

Piling up a great treasure, like a standing army, was also likely to be a source of tension and contribute to the outbreak of war. "The accumulation of treasure in a state would in the same way be regarded by other states as a menace of war, and might compel them to anticipate this by striking the first blow. For of the three forces, the power of arms, the power of alliance, and the power of money, the last might well become the most reliable instrument of war, did not the difficulty of ascertaining the amount stand in the way."[6] It remains to be seen in our own time whether Japan, for example, can use its wealth as a substitute for aggressive arms to achieve its aims of predominance in Asia.

Point 4: "No national debt shall be contracted in connection with the external affairs of the state." Kant approves of the state contracting debt for internal public works—improvement of roads, grain storage, and so on. He saw, however, some of the pernicious effects of debts and credit piling up indefinitely

4. Ibid., 108.
5. Ibid., 108, 109.
6. Ibid., 111.

when creditors did not press their claims all at once. Rulers relying on easy credit were reinforced in their propensity toward war, "an inclination," Kant says, "which seems to be implanted in human nature." This kind of credit system must somehow be terminated as part of the advance toward perpetual peace.[7]

Point 5: "No state shall violently interfere with the constitution and administration of another." This is a reinforcement of the post-Westphalian principle of nonintervention. For Kant, the internal integrity and autonomy of a state is a first principle of international relations. The formation and perpetuity of a republican state is a harbinger of the fulfillment of the goal of perpetual peace and also the best opportunity for the inhabitants to realize themselves as individuals to the full extent of their capacity. "For what can justify it in so doing? . . . The erring state can much more serve as a warning by exemplifying the great evils which a nation draws down on itself through its own lawlessness."[8] The international lawyer Emerich de Vattel, cited by Kant, writes that no foreign power has a right to judge the conduct and administration of any sovereign power. This viewpoint and tradition are part of statism, the treatment of states as the sole arbiters of power. The rise of human rights and environmental issues, calling on natural law and universal standards for support and legitimacy, challenges the sovereignty of the national state.

And the sixth and last point in the first section is: "No state at war with another shall continence such modes of hostility as would make mutual confidence impossible in a subsequent state of peace: such are the employment of assassins or of poisoners, breaches of capitulation, the instigation and making use of treachery in the hostile state." Such practices, Kant believes, are dishonorable. To make peace in the first instance and then to assure its continuation, states must have at least a minimum level of confidence in each other; otherwise, no peace can be concluded and every war will be one of extermination.

> War, however, is only our wretched expedient of averting a right by force, an expedient adopted in the state of nature, where no court of justice exists which could settle the matter in dispute. In circumstances like these, neither of the two parties can be called an unjust enemy, because this form of speech presupposes a legal decision: the issue in the conflict—just as in the case of the so-called Judgment of God—decides on which side a right is. Between states, however, no punitive war (*bellum puniturim*) is thinkable, because between them, a relation of superior and inferior does not exist. Whence it follows that a war of extermination, where the

7. Ibid., 111–12.
8. Ibid., 112–13.

process of annihilation would strike both parties at once and all right as well, would bring about perpetual peace only in the great graveyard of the human race. Such a war, then, and therefore also the use of all means which leads to war must be absolutely forbidden."[9]

The second section of Kant's peace program is titled "Containing the Definitive Articles of a Perpetual Peace between States." He begins by saying: "A state of peace among men who live side by side is not the natural state (*status naturalis*), which is rather to be described as a state of war: That is to say, although there is not perhaps always actual open hostility, yet there is a constant threatening that an outbreak may occur. Thus the state of peace must be established. For the mere cessation of hostilities is no guarantee of continued peaceful relations, and unless this guarantee is given by every individual to his neighbor—which can only be done in a state of society regulated by law—one man is at liberty to challenge another and treat him as an enemy."[10] In his conception of the state of nature as a state of war, Kant is at one with Hobbes in his view of nature as a war of all against all, curbed only by the formation of the state. In exchange for giving up some of his rights for protection by the state, man made his first and dangerous step of preferring order to freedom. Kant's philosophy tries to remedy this problem by establishing a stronger and sounder framework (the republic), which will once again allow man to expand his freedom. The ideal continuation of this process will be a federation of republics (with some qualifications), all with the aim of establishing perpetual peace.

Kant's First Definitive Article of Perpetual Peace states that "the civil constitution of each state shall be republican." This requirement comes from a fundamental element of Kant's philosophy, that is, his contention that the only proposition that is good, without qualification, is that of goodwill. Significant political implications flow from this belief. First, everyone is capable of having goodwill, save perhaps the most depraved of the human race. This means that there is this basis for human equality, and it can best be realized in a republican form. No one is subject to external force and threats to his own autonomy as a free person, willingly serving as a member of this constitutional civil community. "And the only question for us now is, whether it is also the one constitution which can lead to perpetual peace."[11]

Kant was convinced that the monarchical form of government was the bane of peace; a king would plunge into war for profit and personal ambition, con-

9. Ibid., 114–16.
10. Ibid., 117–18.
11. Ibid., 121.

trary to the interest of his subjects, who might well lose their lives and property. They had no vote or veto over the king's decision. In a republic, in contrast, each person was a citizen and not a subject and had a vote and was immediately involved in protecting the community. Compare the status of the citizen to a subject of the monarch in a situation of war or peace: "The monarch can decide to go to war for the most trifling reasons, as if it were a kind of pleasure party. Any justification of it that is necessary for the sake of decency he can leave without concern to the diplomatic corps, who are always only too ready with their services."[12] Machiavelli's *necessito* was alive and well at the turn of the nineteenth century.

Kant distinguishes between the form of the state, based on the differences of rules and sovereignty—monarchy, aristocracy, or democracy—and the form of government. The form is based on the constitution, "itself the act of that universal will which transforms a multitude into a nation." On this premise, the form is either republican or despotic. "Republicanism is the political principle of severing the executive power of the government from the legislative. Despotism is that principle in the pursuance of which the state arbitrarily puts into effect laws which it has made: consequently, it is the administration of the public will, but this is identical with the private will of the ruler." Kant is opposed to democracy because it is a despotic form of government, relying only on a majority for its sovereignty, creating a situation in which "the universal will is in contradiction with itself and with the principle of freedom."[13]

For Kant there was only one way to avoid despotism and that was through a republican form of government. Such a government is in accordance with the "idea of right." Only republicanism, with its separate (and superior) legislator and executive will avoid the risk of conflating the two branches plus the judiciary into one executive. "This kind of representative government is the sturdiest vessel to contain the contents of perpetual peace."[14]

Now we turn to the Second Definitive Article of Perpetual Peace: "The law of nations shall be founded on a federation of free states." Here Kant grapples with the problems of the force and sanction of international law, how relations between sovereign states can approach a condition central to civil society through a regular, dependable enforcement mechanism. "The depravity of human nature shows itself without disguise in the unrestrained relations of nations to each other, while in the law governed civil state, much of this is hidden

12. Ibid., 123.
13. Ibid., 125.
14. Ibid., 120–28.

by the check of government. This being so, it is astonishing that the word 'right' has not yet been entirely banished from the politics of war as pedantic, and that no state has yet ventured to publicly advocate this point of view. For Hugo Grotius, Pufendorf, Vattel and others—Job's comforters, all of them—are always quoted in good faith to justify an attack, although their codes, whether couched in philosophical or diplomatic terms have not—nor can have—the slightest legal force, because states as such, are under no common external authority; and there is no instance of a state having ever been moved to argument to desist from its purpose even when this was backed up by the testimony of such great men."[15]

Kant then goes on to justify his otherwise quixotic search for perpetual peace, beyond the simple fact that such is our individual and collective duty. "This homage which every state renders—in words at least—to the idea of right, proves that, although it may be slumbering, there is, notwithstanding, to be found in man a still higher natural moral capacity by the aid of which he will in time gain the mastery over the evil principle in his nature, the existence of which he is unable to deny."[16]

At the present time, Kant writes, there is no other way for states to pursue their external claims to a particular right than war. This situation remains essentially the same to this day and for the same reason: no superior external tribunal, that is, a freestanding judiciary outside of the state system, exists, including the UN. The International Court of Justice can hear only those cases that the member states agree to present. This situation prevails, despite another two hundred years of effort. (Modern schemes toward world order will be considered later.) A peace treaty may settle a particular war, Kant argued (not necessarily in reference to justice), but the conditions allowing more wars are not addressed. Here Kant proposes a "covenant of peace" that "would seek to put an end to war forever," even though he acknowledges mankind's apparent preference for disorder. Kant is convinced of the merit of a federation of republican states leading to this goal of peace. It is a simple step then for the people to say, "We shall form ourselves into a state, that is to say, constitute for ourselves a supreme legislature, administrative and judicial power which will settle our disputes peacefully."[17] Forming such a state changes the dispute from one of external sovereignty between sovereign states, with no external authority, to one representing the domestic scene in a normative state.

15. Ibid., 131–32.
16. Ibid., 132.
17. Ibid., 135.

The reluctance so far of states to give up their sovereignty to become a united superstate has proven to be formidable. In this century, efforts to minimize or to avoid the issue of sovereignty are represented by the League of Nations and the United Nations. A campaign to overcome national sovereignty was launched during the middle of World War II by an American, Clarence Streit. He wrote a book, *Union Now: A Proposal for a Federal Union of the Democracies of the North Atlantic*, which proposed an Atlantic union, which, under the Kantian thrall, would gradually expand until it became a worldwide federation.[18] The idea of a world government had a certain cachet after World War II, at least on university and college campuses. It still has chapters here and there, but the disabilities of such a conclusion are so widely recognized that it has little credibility as an international political alternative.

The Third Definitive Article of Perpetual Peace states: "The rights of man, as citizens of the world, shall be limited to the conditions of universal hospitality." This at first strikes one as a marginal concern, yet from the Kantian perspective, if nations will not treat each other's citizens with minimum courtesy and concern for their liberty and protection, then the prospects for establishing a fraternity of nations become less likely. Kant is critical of the conduct of China and Japan toward non-nationals, such as preventing Europeans from entering their countries to conduct business or to proselytize their citizens. And the growing European practice of colonization, taking over other nations as if no one owned the land by natural right, or training such native peoples for military service, using them as means to European ends, earned Kant's rebuke. A violation of one person's rights somewhere is a violation of a common right everywhere. "Hence the idea of a cosmopolitan right is no fantastical, high-flown notion of right, but a complement of the unwritten code of law—necessary for the public rights of mankind in general and thus for the realization of perpetual peace. For only by endeavoring to fulfill the conditions laid down by the cosmopolitan law can we flatter ourselves that we are gradually approaching that ideal."[19] This position resonates well with today's concerns over human rights, and the division between those favoring universal versus particular rights.

Kant, having completed his essay on perpetual peace, went on to write two supplements and two appendixes to make more specific how mankind in general and well-meaning governments in particular might make progress toward his grand goal. He muses over the apparent fact that war is engrafted in some

18. Clarence Streit, *Union Now: A Proposal for a Federal Union of the Democracies of the North Atlantic* (New York: Harper and Brothers, 1938).

19. Kant, *Perpetual Peace,* 137, 142.

way on human nature and is even in some quarters regarded as noble in itself: "Some seem inspired by the love of glory aside from nature or self-interest."[20] He then lists some observations relevant to this point.

First, "Even if a people were not compelled through internal discord to submit to the restraint of public laws, war would bring this about, working from without."[21] There is always another tribe somewhere about as a perennial source of potential conflict. Second,

> The idea of international law presupposes the separate existence of a number of neighborhood and independent states; and, although such a condition of things is in itself already a state of war (if a federative union of these nations does not prevent the outbreak of hostilities) yet, according to the idea of reason, this is better than that all the states should be merged into one under a power which has gained the ascendancy over its neighbors and gradually becomes a universal monarchy. For the wider the sphere of their jurisdiction, the more laws lose in force; and soulless despotism, when it has choked the seeds of good, at last sinks into anarchy. Nevertheless, it is the desire of every state, or of its ruler, to attain to a permanent condition of peace, in this very way, that is to say, by subjecting the whole world as far as possible to its sway. But nature wills it otherwise, and prevents them from intermixing: namely, the difference of language and religion.[22]

A certain homogeneity was essential to Kant for the creation and sustenance of a state.

Third, "As nature wisely separates nations which the will of each state, mentioned even by the principle of international law, would gladly unite under its own sway by stratagem or force; in the same way, on the other hand, she unites nations when the principle of cosmopolitan right would not have secured against violence and war." Another trend supporting peace, Kant notes, is the ever-increasing commercial ties between various states which generate wealth. "Commercial spirit cannot co-exist with war, and sooner or later it takes possession of every nation."[23] This prospect has often been cited since—and especially before World War I—as a promising trend that ensured peace among nations.

What are we to make of the idealistic argument in general and the Kantian approach to perpetual peace in particular? As Sissela Bok's article on perpetual peace demonstrated, there were powerful countertrends from Machiavellian

20. Ibid., 151.
21. Ibid., 152.
22. Ibid., 155–56.
23. Ibid., 157.

politics ascending to the raison d'état that followed in the time of Richelieu and Metternich. The works of Erasmus mentioned by Bok in their pacifist character ironically found their staunchest opponent in the Catholic Church. This will be clear in Chapter 6 when we review the just war tradition and that church's preference not to try to eliminate war altogether, but rather to settle for restricting war and trying to channel it into practices that would give the Church a role in the secular world as well as in the superior spiritual world. Bok's argument that the idealist approach to peace is a sensible and powerful one cannot be ignored; many find her position convincing. This argument will remain with us through the book as the realist-idealist paradigm raises its head at important moments.

Kant is one of the more complex as well as important philosophers we shall encounter. He was much influenced in his international philosophy by both the American and French Revolutions. He often is an opaque philosopher, relying for his arguments on metaphysics, based on his insights beyond reason, to explain the origin and nature of his philosophy. For example, like Plato, he looks at the world as having two parts, the phenomenal, or the world open to our sight and perceptions, and the noumenal, the world of reality that we can barely contemplate in our minds. These two worlds come together because of an innate destiny based on the teleological predetermination that says these two pictures will be united. This then gives one a picture of the moral and physical world and the freedom and autonomy to pursue one's life. Such metaphysics is not the primary concern of this book. Perpetual peace for Kant is a process involving four principles: (1) goodwill, accessible to us all, is the only absolute good; (2) from this single good, men naturally aspire to a republican form of government; (3) such a government, with its iron separation of powers— legislative, executive, and judicial—provides a government wherein each citizen can fulfill his or her potential; and one of the attributes of this kind of citizen is (4) a duty to pursue universal peace. This is the basic package of the Kantian international relations program. So this quest for peace was one of the obligations and duties that Kant saw as key elements of his categorical imperative, the greatest of which was his maxim that all of us must treat each other as ends in ourselves and not simply as means, and that even though this sometimes fails, we must pursue this goal, for such is our duty.

With *Perpetual Peace*, Kant is properly placed in the category of idealists, those who strive for goals that seem beyond our reach. (Martin Wight, as I have noted, lists Kant as a revolutionary.) But Kant's basic philosophy of human nature is nonetheless supportive of the three-part canon of historical realism, embracing as Kant does the concept of interest, the natural tendency for conflict, and the role of morality in this world. To overcome human nature, Kant had faith in republican government as the device to establish peace. Here he equated peace with an institution; Erasmus and other religious philosophers naturally relied on faith and the changing of man's heart as the way of peace. Kant introduced the idea of an institutional change, the creation of republics, to do the job. This was at the opening of the nineteenth century; before the century was out, one of his spiritual followers, Marx, was convinced that economic determinism would remake the world, and though mankind at least in the short term would follow the path of realism, man's evil nature would be thwarted by the unleashing of historical forces that would transform contemporary man into the new "socialist man." Another follower, Hegel, thought that the spirit of freedom would ensure the triumph of liberal democracy, without regard to man's nature. Mankind would have to yield to these historic forces, and peace would come about despite the present nature of mankind. All of this will be explored in detail in Chapter 5.

We will now, however, proceed to a consideration of a quite different perspective on the problem of relations among states as we turn to a different philosophy and different interpretations. We will focus on whether the tenets of historical realism hold up under the challenge of the Chinese Empire. What principles were incompatible, beginning with those of the Treaty of Westphalia, and which ones were similar?

4   China's International Relations System

The contrast between Kant and the classical realists mainly rests on his hopes for institutional change, not for a major overhaul of the human condition. Kant's appreciation of the evil of human nature was not significantly different from that of either Thucydides or Machiavelli. This encapsulates the progression of realism in the West up through the nineteenth century. In the meantime, on the other side of the globe, the Western system of international relations had come up against an enigmatic opponent of its view, the Chinese Empire. Here also was a test for the proposition that human nature was universal, that beneath different customs and philosophies, political man was everywhere recognizable. One way to conduct this test is to follow the course of an Asian country, Korea, as it journeyed through Chinese international relations as a member of the Chinese tributary system, its version of international politics. The history is revealing as to how the Chinese world worked and may be illustrative about what to expect of China in the future, thereby providing a valuable guide for future American foreign policy.[1]

During its centuries-long association and intercourse with China, Korea had managed through much sacrifice of blood and treasure to maintain its hold over the Korean peninsula. At times, under the strong Silla dynasty (A.D. 668–935) and in times of able kings and prosperity, it extended its reach over large areas of Manchuria as well. But by and large, the Koreans, after their long immigration from Central Asia, were content to stay on the peninsula. This offered them a degree of security and the possibility of solidifying their culture and way of life and maintaining their independence in a dangerous and hostile world.

1. For background, see, for example, John K. Fairbank, Edwin O. Reischauer, and Albert M. Craig, *East Asia: Tradition and Transformation* (Boston: Houghton Mifflin, 1973), Chaps. 11 and 12.

China in the beginning was the local hegemon, and the Koreans conveniently fell under the sway of the Chinese tributary system, which regulated interstate relations along China's immense periphery.[2] China early on saw itself as the "Middle Kingdom," based first on geography but above all on the cultural cohesion and superiority of the Chinese (*Han*) race. The first emperor to succeed in unifying the contending kingdoms or feudal states was the famous Chin Shih Huang-ti, who in 221 B.C. united China. This was the time of the construction of the Great Wall north of his capital city of Chang An (Long Peace, now Hsian), and upon his death in 210 B.C., it was the occasion for the making of the burial grounds of the porcelain army that have rightly gained fame and admiration over the past two decades.

In an intellectual sense, the Ch'in dynasty was marked by the efforts of the emperor and his nobles to eliminate the Confucian texts and learning, with their emphasis on virtue and accommodation, in favor of the Legalists. This was an attempt to establish law rather than the ceremonies and rites of Confucianism as the pillar of government and its preeminence over interpersonal hierarchical relationships. Although classical texts were indeed burned, Confucianism nonetheless survived this assault, and the ascendancy of the Legalists came to an end; the Legalist approach to government and society failed and has not fully recovered in modern times. Confucianism has undergone reform and repair but still undergirds Chinese domestic society as well as the Chinese view of the world.[3]

The tributary system at first grew out of the imperial desire to deal differently with clans and tribes that were not Han, those who were culturally inferior or different from the dominant group, and establish a hierarchical relationship with them. The vassal had to acknowledge the superior position of the Han emperor, and a system of embassies and rites was developed to handle this inferior-superior relationship. As this system came to fruition in the seventeenth and eighteenth centuries, it added a strong commercial and trade element that became more important than the symbolic vassal role. Korea was an important actor in this system from the outset, around 200 B.C. during the Han dynasty (206 B.C. to A.D. 220). The Koreans acquiesced to this tributary role for three reasons. First was the reality of power. If they refused to pay homage to the Chinese emperor and his Middle Kingdom, China might assert its power and take over militarily. Second, the Koreans admired the Chinese culture, and

2. Ibid., 197–99.

3. See, however, Thomas Metzger, "Transcending the West" (Hoover Institution, Stanford University, 1996), for his view that Maoism is becoming the new Chinese ideology.

they acknowledged Chinese superiority—as did the other weaker members of the tributary system—and accepted an inferior hierarchical status. Finally, there were advantages to being on good terms with China, including having a claim on Chinese military support in time of need. For centuries—despite occasional clashes with China, particularly over settlements in Manchuria—the system served both sides well. Yet toward the end of the nineteenth century, the tributary system proved to be a liability for Korea and was a factor in its temporary disappearance from the international scene.

It is worth spending a bit of time explaining how the Chinese world worked in general before describing Korea's experience, particularly with regard to the destruction of the system, because China has reemerged in the late twentieth century as a principal world power and vestiges of its traditional worldview will once again be a factor to ponder in world politics. Since the Han dynasty, according to Kenneth Scott Latourette, "the state has usually been based upon Confucian principles modified to meet the exigencies of changing conditions."[4] Confucius promoted a series of virtues that governed the role of the individual in Chinese society as well as his view of the outside world in general. A few samples from his philosophy will suffice to give a sense of these ideas and how they served as a basis for the Middle Kingdom in its relations with non-Chinese culture and alien states.

Four principal virtues will be considered. The first is *Jen*, which means "fellow feeling," a notion of the personal and societal bond between individuals and, by extension, between groups and even nations. In one place Confucius says, "Unyielding fortitude and simple modesty approaches *Jen*." One can observe someone with these attributes "outside the home [treat people] as if receiving a guest; employ the people as if performing a great sacrifice. That which one does not desire, do not do to other people. Dwelling in a feudal lord's state, he lacks resentment. Dwelling in a great officer's estate, he lacks ill-will."[5] A person with this virtue, demonstrated by his own actions, clearly would set a good example for interstate relations. A related virtue is *Li*, which literally means the rules of propriety for ceremonies. But philosophically speaking, it has the sense of inner sincerity and virtue, an idealized way of how the Middle Kingdom wished to maintain good relations with its vassals; it was hoped that after long association with the Han society, some of the vassals would reach a

4. Kenneth Scott Latourette, *The Chinese: Their History and Culture*, 3d rev. ed. (New York: Macmillan, 1946), 518.

5. James Legge, "Confucian Analects," in Vol. 1 of *The Chinese Classics* (London: Thubner, 1861), Book 4, Chap. 16, p. 34.

level of culture that would allow them to be full-fledged members of the Middle Kingdom. This was in fact how the Chinese Empire was consolidated inside the country, but it was difficult, despite *Jen* and *Li*, for non-Chinese to be admitted to the core.

A third virtue is *I*, or righteousness. This term expresses the correct conduct of the individual in all social relationships. It includes the meaning of appropriateness and, extended, becomes a standard for an actor. The Confucian in his daily activities decides first of all which course is *I*. Discovering it, he proceeds directly along that line, regardless of material consequences.[6] "The mind of the superior man is conversant with righteousness; the mind of the mean man is conversant with gain." In political life *I* becomes particularly significant. "A superior man takes office, and performs the righteous duties belonging to it. As to the failure of right principles to make progress, he is aware of that."[7] Righteousness, then, is the only criterion for personal and political practice.

The final Confucian virtue of relevance for the background philosophy of the tributary system is the *Tao*, the proper way to behave and act. In the *Lun Yu* (the Analects), "The Master said, 'the Chun tze' [superior man] is easy to serve and difficult to please; if one pleases him not according to the Tao, he is not pleased."[8] For Confucius, the *Tao* seems to mean an ideal way of government which has an existence of its own, just as "truth" and "beauty" have for many of us an independent existence. Uniting these ideas with the already existing family pattern, Confucius's philosophical theory reached beyond the family to more distant social ties.

This, then, was the philosophical underpinning of the Chinese worldview and of how China wished, in theory, to conduct its relationship with the tribes and nations along its vast periphery. The ceremonial exchange of embassies from time to time, according to the schedule maintained by the court in Beijing, satisfied the Chinese claim as the Middle Kingdom. The tribute missions acknowledged their inferiority in the Chinese hierarchical world. They often received gifts of greater value than they gave. Over time, these tribute missions became poorly concealed trading enterprises, when China was officially not engaged in foreign trade.

This system made it unnecessary for China to station troops in these tributaries, except to control occasional power struggles and civil wars or when the

---

6. See Fung Yu-lan, *A History of Chinese Philosophy*, trans. Dirk Bodde (Beijing: Henri Vetch, 1937), 73–75.

7. Legge, "Confucian Analects," Book 18, Chap. 7, pp. 199–200.

8. Ibid., Book 13, Chap. 25, pp. 137–38.

dependency misbehaved in some way, such as the Korean expansion into Manchuria during the Silla dynasty. (In later years, Machiavelli pointed out in *The Prince* his preference for not going to the expense of having to occupy other principalities.) The Chinese tributary system provided a buffer as well from the onslaughts of foreigners, and China responded to these incursions as required. During the eighteenth and nineteenth centuries, the strain on the Chinese system became severe. Western imperialism, with its superior military technology, proved to be impervious to Chinese defenses, both intellectually and militarily and through the tributary system. Power proved to be the great equalizer.

The Chinese were largely ignorant of the Western system of international relations, assuming that their own hierarchical order was universal and correct, that some states were clearly superior to and stronger than their neighbors. In the meantime, the West was moving in a different direction. The Treaty of Westphalia in 1648, marking the end of the religious wars in Europe, established the principle of the sovereign equality of states. State sovereignty was pronounced inviolate. A second principle was the rule of international law, based on common consent. Agreed-upon laws were binding on the international community (although expediency and not law often determined the hard cases). Third, and perhaps most important, was the recognition by all powers of the importance of the balance of power for their status and security in the world. Properly functioning, this balance would preserve the independence of the states within the European community and ensure that no one state could emerge as the hegemon. It was with these three ideas that the Western powers began to confront the Chinese Empire and its dependencies. A study of the case of Korea, one of first and last and loyal dependencies, will reveal the outcome of this unequal struggle for power in Asia.

China's long tributary relationship with Korea displays more of the power modalities of that enterprise than it does the more idealized Confucian version of one big happy family. One Chinese writer at a time when the West was criticized for its "unequal" treatment of China (1926) said: "Certainly the Chinese once pursued a policy as aggressive as many of the foreign powers are pursuing now. It must be admitted that the foreign powers have been no harsher to China than China was to the surrounding tribes and kingdoms in the Han period."[9] Others describe the Han chastising of Korea in 108 B.C. as "little more than aggression."[10] Later, during the collapse of the Mongol dynasty (1280–

---

9. Wu Hung-chu, "China's Attitude towards Foreign Nations and Nationals Historically Considered," *Chinese Social and Political Science Review* 10 (January 1926): 23.

10. M. Frederick Nelson, *Korea and the Old Orders in Eastern Asia* (Baton Rouge: Louisiana State University Press, 1945), 89.

1368) and the ascension of the Ming, Korea, although accepting Chinese sovereignty, played a role in its northern territory that is difficult to reconcile with
Confucian principles. Taking advantage of the power vacuum south of the Yalu
River, Korean general Li Ch'eng-kuei advanced into this area occupied by the
sinicized Nu-chin tribes, bestowing investitures on them.[11] After Li (in Korean,
Yi, the founder of the Chosun or Yi dynasty, 1392–1911) established himself as
king of the peninsula in A.D. 1391, he further extended Korean administration,
even though his policy was counter to the desires of his suzerain, the Ming government. The Ming rulers intended to place the Nu-chins and all northern
Korea under their jurisdiction. The Ming emperor Ch'ing tzu (1403–24) vigorously conducted the Nu-chin affair, obtaining the allegiance of eleven tribes in
northern Korea, despite secret countermoves on the part of the Koreans. Only
when it became obvious that their plans would not succeed did the Koreans pe-
tition Ch'ing-tzu for the right to govern the territory of the Nu-chins south of
the Tumen River. The request was granted, China abandoning claims to territory south of the Tumen and the Koreans giving up active aspirations for
northern lands.

Confucian dogma was susceptible to interpretation: action that ordinarily
might be considered immoral could be justified through the ideology. When
the Chinese dealt with people who did not understand the principle of *Li,* they
had to use force to reach a common denominator. In fact, Confucius himself
upheld "benevolent" imperialism in the sense that he believed in influencing
backward people in the ways of progress. The prevention of tyranny and abso-
lutism was a legitimate function of benevolent government. After the overthrow
of a tyrant, if the people desired it, their state could become a member of the
Chinese system without violating the ethical rules. Immoral and bad government are also suitable prey for benevolence. There was, then, a fine but definite
line of distinction between "benevolent" imperialism and plain imperialism.

This tension between the ideal and the practical, the ambivalence between
theory and practice, is captured perfectly in this statement of Wang An-shih in
the Sung dynasty: "It is quite true that the use of military force to strengthen
the state is not the ideal way. A wise ruler should alternate between mild measures and strong measures. Although force should never be the only consideration, it is at present absolutely necessary for the preservation of the state. The
ancient rulers held armed forces in high esteem and at the same time taught

---

11. T. C. Lin, "Manchuria in the Ming Empire," *Nankei Social and Economic Quarterly* 8 (April
1935): 1–43.

moral principles to the people. These two policies—government by force, and government by ethics—may be consistently combined."[12]

In brief, the tributary system might be compared to a large but flawed diamond; it contained imperfections and displayed many facets. According to J. K. Fairbank and S. Y. Teng, "The tributary system was a framework within which all sorts of interests, personal and imperial, economic and social found expression." Further, "There was an interplay between greed and statecraft, dynastic policy and vested interest, similar to that in any great political institution." Or, put another way, it was a system based on an ethical code that determined the form of interstate intercourse; this form, as an ideology, held Chinese international relations to a course of conduct that, although not attaining the ideal, could be explained and perhaps justified by Confucian moral principles. This had an important result. Chinese political and military power over the tributaries was, if not disguised, considerably moderated by adherence to the Confucian pattern: "The later Ch'ing rulers appear to have covered the tributary relationships with a sugar coating heavy enough to make it decidedly palatable."[13]

The reason it is worthwhile recreating and reexploring the lost world of the Chinese tributary system in the context of Korea is that it had a profound and disastrous effect on Korea's future at the end of the nineteenth century which inexorably shaped the nation's fate in the twentieth century. The United States found itself in 1950 as an unwitting inheritor of this past. And it is worth remembering China's own view of itself in international relations, as its power once again is rising in the Middle Kingdom and will be increasingly on display in the twenty-first century, as it was, for example, in the case of Taiwan at the end of the present century. (See the Conclusion for a discussion of China's role in international politics in the twenty-first century.)

The early contacts between East and West did not seriously disturb the old Chinese order. Western traders on official missions from 1655 to 1795 generally followed the Chinese preference, kowtowing (knocking the head on the floor) when attending an audience with the emperor and bringing gifts (tribute) in the framework of trade. In the eighteenth century, however, the Chinese began to concentrate trade in Canton and to give a monopoly to the *co-hong*, who supervised trade with the Western powers. Irritated by this system and the arrogance of the Chinese officials, the British as the leading trading power began to

---

12. Lin Mou-shêng, *Men and Ideas: An Informal History of Chinese Political Thought* (New York: John Day, 1942), 120.

13. J. K. Fairbank and S. Y. Teng, "On the Ch'ing Tributary System," *Harvard Journal of Asiatic Studies* 1 (1941): 141, 160.

press China to behave like a Western nation on a basis of equality and with due regard to the Western state system based on sovereign equality, international law, and a sense of participation in the Western community.

The British reaction on coming up against imperial China was to denounce it as an uncivilized state:

> China, however disposed its rulers may be to deny this fact, is one of a community of nations with common rights and obligations, and any claim to exemption from the recognized terms of national intercourse is inadequate in the interest of all other countries. To admit such a right of exemption would be to allow the arrogant superiority in power and civilization, and to pamper the hostile conceit of her people.
>
> So long as the sovereign states of Europe will permit so obvious an inference it cannot be a matter of surprise, and scarcely subject of reproach to the Chinese, that they should be so ready to assert and so pertinacious in acting upon it.
>
> But even if exclusion from the territories, from all trade and intercourse were an absolute right in the first instance, the Chinese have forfeited all claim to its exercise—first, by voluntarily entering into relations political and commercial in ages past with other States and people, by exchange of embassies, by opening their ports and territories and encouraging trade; and secondly, by aggressive wars and invasions of the territory of Europe by the Tartar and Mongolian races who have ruled the country.
>
> China preserves her undoubted rights of self-preservation as a political society and an empire, but this does not involve the incidental right of interdictory intercourse, because the right of decision must be shared by the interdicted party.[14]

This passage demonstrates that Western states, like the Chinese, believed their method of international intercourse conformed to nature and reason, and they therefore erected it into a universal. The English, imbued with the accomplishments of their own culture, which was blooming in the Age of Enlightenment, were amazed and chagrined at the attitude of the Chinese; action against the Chinese was rationalized on the basis of the Western doctrine of international relations. Elijah Coleman Bridgman pointed out that in the relations of China to the Western trading nations, "Negotiations becoming the character of great and independent nations, seem never to have been undertaken." The Chinese simply enroll these Western nations as tribute bearers, who have, therefore, "frequently been treated with neglect and indignity; and after all have effected little or nothing for the benefit of those who sent them, or for the world."

---

14. See H. F. MacNair, ed., *Modern Chinese History: Selected Readings* (Shanghai: Commercial Press, 1927), 17.

Furthermore, the Chinese "practically deny the existence of relative rights among nations," believing that the emperor holds sway throughout the world.

> In this assumption of all right and dominion, foreigners have acquiesced. This acquiescence has grown out of the doctrine (very prevalent in the west), that nations have a right to manage their own affairs in their own way, and have no responsibilities in reference to other portions of the human family; and that so long as one permits intercourse in a way it chooses, and refuses to interfere in any other way, or interdicts it altogether, other nations have no right to interfere or complain. . . . The doctrine is equally opposed to the law of God, to reason, and to common sense. Ignorance, superstition, pride, and ambition have acted jointly to strengthen, establish, and perpetuate it.[15]

Bridgman concludes that the Western powers must, therefore, force China to cooperate in the Western family of nations.[16] England, intoxicated by its own power and prestige and proud of its commercial and colonizing success, believed it would be good for China to share in its beneficent influence. Thus we have a mirror-image conundrum as China and England look out on the world and see only themselves.

Now if the Europeans did not understand the Chinese international state system, the Chinese were even more uninformed about the West. The Koreans at this juncture were not yet directly involved in these matters, but unfortunately, toward the end of the nineteenth century, they were no better prepared for this contest than the Chinese, who took this approach. The Chinese emperor, after receiving the British Macartney embassy at Jehol in 1793, issued a mandate, which read in part:

> You, o King, live beyond the confines of many seas; nevertheless, impelled by your humble desire to partake of the benefits of our civilization, you have dispatched a mission respectfully bearing your memorial. Your Envoy has crossed the seas and paid his respects at my Court on the anniversary of my birthday. To show your devotion, you have also sent offerings of your country's produce.
>
> I have perused your memorial; the earnest terms in which it is couched reveal respectful humility on your part, which is highly praiseworthy. In consideration of the fact that your Ambassador and his deputy have come a long way with your memorial and tribute, I have shown high favour and have allowed them to be introduced into my presence.
>
> Swaying the wide world, I have but one aim in view, namely, to maintain a per-

---

15. *Chinese Repository*, 20 vols. (Canton, printed for the proprietors, 1835), 3:417, 419.

16. E. R. Hughes, *The Invasion of China by the Western World* (London: A. and C. Black, 1937), 102.

fect governance and to fulfill the duties of the State: strange and costly objects do not interest me. If I have commanded that the tribute offerings sent by you, O King, are to be accepted, this was solely in consideration for the spirit which prompted you to dispatch them from afar. Our dynasty's majestic virtue has penetrated unto every country under Heaven, and Kings of all nations have offered their costly tribute by land and sea. . . . It behooves you, O King, to respect my sentiments and to display even greater.devotion and loyalty in future, so that, by perpetual submission to our Throne, you may secure peace and prosperity for your country hereafter. Besides making gifts (of which I enclose an inventory) to each member of your Mission, I confer upon you, O King, valuable presents in excess of the number usually bestowed on such occasions, including silks and curios—a list of which is likewise enclosed. Do you reverently receive them and take a note of my tender goodwill toward you! A special mandate.[17]

From these examples, the incompatibility of the two systems was evident, and the outcome was not decided by superior moral philosophy but rather by commercial and military technology. China reluctantly signed various treaties with the Western powers, such as the Treaty of Nanking in 1845, by which the Chinese technically (but not spiritually) recognized that they were on an equal footing with the Western countries. China continued to hope that its fortunes would improve and that internal reforms, based on adapting Western technology to its own needs while retaining its unique culture and philosophy, would turn the tide.

If the equality of states was the theoretical basis for the breakup of the Confucian state system, the Western idea of sovereignty, misunderstood by the Chinese, was the practical principle that undermined the tributary system. For the Chinese to accept other nations as equals would have meant recognizing equality of virtue and culture and, consequently, the destruction of the Chinese worldview. The satellite states had for centuries been attracted to the Chinese cultural core like iron filings to a magnet. In the absence of counterattraction, the interacting system of mutual obligations and benefits whirled in an undeviating orbit. The impingement of the Western state system on the Confucian community, proclaiming the sovereign equality of states, was literally a worldshaking blow. The Chinese conception of the preordained harmony of natural and social patterns where all things had a definite and proper place was challenged by this revolutionary doctrine.[18] Forced by Western arms to accept the

17. E. Backhouse and J. O. P. Bland, *Annuals and Memoirs of the Court of Peking* (Boston: Houghton Mifflin, 1914), 324–25.

18. Latourette, *The Chinese*, 525–26.

principle of equality, the Chinese, after a series of military and diplomatic defeats, watched their tributary system disintegrate. Ironically, the Liu Ch'iu islands, under pressure from the Japanese, wholehearted converts to the Western system, especially vis-à-vis China, were the first tributary to be drawn from Chinese control in 1872. Although the Liu Ch'iu islands in themselves were of small account, the principle involved was enormous and set the stage for the destruction of the whole system, notably exemplified by the case of Korea. The separation of Korea from the Chinese state system will serve to highlight the principles and operations of both international orders.

With cultural contacts as well as military ones dating back to the early Han dynasty (111 B.C. to A.D. 100), the Koreans by propinquity were in the Chinese orbit and were generally content for centuries to stay in it. In the end, it was with great reluctance that Korea left the tributary system that had served it well. Now a new danger was posed without precedent. Because the Western powers did not comprehend the principles of the Confucian state system, they were confused over the status of Korea. This confusion played into the hands of the Japanese, who understood the situation perfectly. Western international law did not supply a definition for, or recognize, such a nebulous term as *shu pang*, or "dependent state." The Korean dilemma was not easily resolved; the Koreans tried to play this ambiguity to their own benefit, but this effort worked against them. As Frederick Nelson put it, "With the coming of the West, Korea attempted to maintain a double status, being simultaneously in the disintegrating East Asiatic system and in the ascendant system of the West."[19]

Korea had isolated itself from all foreign intercourse except with its suzerain. By 1846, however, the French were attempting to force their way into Korea, but were unsuccessful. Finally, in 1876, Japan signed a treaty of amity and commerce with Korea. In this document Korea agreed that it was as independent and sovereign as Japan, thereby, from the position of Western international law, disavowing Chinese overlordship. The Chinese government, anxious to avoid any more difficulties with the newest member of the West, did not press its claim as suzerain over Korea, and as in the Liu Ch'iu incident, the failure of the Chinese to comprehend the significance of sovereignty undermined their position in Korea. After the Korean-Japanese treaty, the Western nations had to decide whether to recognize Korea as an independent nation or to accept the evasive Chinese assertion of suzerainty. In a letter from the king of Korea to the president of the United States, which was to accompany the Korean-American treaty of 1882, the confusion, paradoxically, was clearly expressed: "The King of

19. Nelson, *Korea and the Old Order*, xiv.

Corea acknowledges that Corea is a tributary of China, and in regard to both internal administration and foreign intercourse, it enjoys complete independence."[20]

Contradictory as this statement might seem, it describes the precise relationship of China and Korea. According to the Confucian dogma, the parent, China, did not interfere in either the internal or external affairs of its *shu pang* except, as with a family, in times of crisis. The Western nations, however, taking a cue from the clause in the Japanese treaty and desirous of placing responsibility for signing the treaty on Korea, decide to consider Korea an independent state. In the succeeding four years, England, Germany, Italy, Russia, and France signed treaties with Korea, all based on the Japanese model.[21]

Although the damage had already been done, Li Hung-chang, the Chinese statesman most responsible for Chinese relations with Korea, attempted to strengthen ties between the two countries. He sent the Chinese general Yuan Shih-kai to Korea to consolidate the ancient Chinese position as surrogate. This move was moderately successful, in spite of Russian and Japanese opposition. In 1882, for example, the Chinese intervened in Korea, seizing the Tai-wun-kun, the regent, and restoring the Yi dynasty king. China then concluded a commercial agreement that openly asserted the Confucian superior-inferior relationship.[22] After this display, the Western powers began to question Korean independence (in view of the lack of Japanese protests at this intervention) and the validity of treaties with Korea which were made without the approval of the Chinese emperor. Li Hung-chang exercised control that the Westerners would recognize, although still using the traditional relationship. He also added a new element to his policy by employing Chinese commercial agents in Korea, who could function under dual roles. Japan, however, overthrew the Chinese position in Korea as a result of the Sino-Japanese War of 1894–95 and finally settled the matter for thirty-five years by annexing Korea in 1910. In this way, China, humiliated and reduced to a subcolony, became a member of the Western state system. Korea had many difficult times yet to endure.

Despite the injunctions of Confucius and the high-blown tones of the imperial rescripts, China's thrusts and parries with its Western tormentors reveal a leadership completely alert to interest and power as motivating factors and a re-

20. See Statistical Department of the Inspector General of Customs, *Treaties, Regulations etc. between Corea and Other Powers* (Shanghai, 1891), 41–50.

21. Harold M. Vinacke, *A History of the Far East in Modern Times*, 2d rev. ed. (New York: F. S. Crofts, 1937), 115.

22. See Nelson, *Korea and the Old Order*, 152.

course to morality as a legitimizing principle of international relations. China tried to deal with the Western state system in a superior role as a great empire and civilization. But finally it was forced to respond as a sovereign state, as only an equal member of the Western community. For the first half of the twentieth century, it tried to become an equal to the principal Western powers. Its efforts were frustrated by the affronts of the West and undermined by internal strife, civil wars, and foreign invasion, particularly from Japan. The "unequal treaties" imposed on China by the West were one of the burdens borne by Chiang Kai-shek during World War II as China strove to become one of the Big Five of the UN Security Council.

Part of the reason for the success of the communist revolution in China was precisely the perceived weakness of China on the international scene that propelled Mao Tse-tung to the fore in October 1949. China was driven internationally to regain the respect and prestige that it had lost during its long period of humiliation and entered the Korean War in 1950 in part to demonstrate that it was the revolutionary leader of Asia. China is still dissatisfied with the way the United States deals with it, somewhat short of the equal treatment it expects and insists upon. As in the United States, Chinese politics are driven by interest, power, and a moral view of the world. How these aspirations will be worked out, what will be the moral content of the reconciliation, is still unknown.

Today, even among sinologists dedicated to promoting the uniqueness of their product, there is growing recognition that China, in its international politics, actually follows the principles of realism rather than the flowering axioms of Sun Tze in his *Art of War*. Alastair Ian Johnston, in *Cultural Realism: Strategic Culture and Grand Strategy in Chinese History*, makes the case for Chinese realism in its conduct of international relations.[23] Arthur Waldron, in his review of this book, states that "new and archivally based accounts of the Korean War have established just how involved China was, and how far from mere 'signaling' were its military objectives. There have been re-examinations of domestic policy that show power rather than ideology to have been the key factor."[24]

Johnston's book points up the distinction between Confucian theory and Chinese political practice. This is relevant, in my view, to an appreciation of the goals of current Chinese rearmament programs, based in part on the bargain sale procurement of technologically advanced Russian military equipment. "To

23. Alastair Ian Johnston, *Cultural Realism: Strategic Culture and Grand Strategy in Chinese History* (Princeton: Princeton University Press, 1997).

24. Arthur Waldron, review of *Cultural Realism: Strategic Culture and Grand Strategy in Chinese History*, by Alastair Ian Johnston, *The New Republic*, 22 June 1997, 36–41, quote on 39.

the question of what China intends to do with the new military capabilities that it is acquiring, Johnston's implicit answer is, clearly, use them. While some observers still talk about China's pride, its requirements for prestige, its desire to overcome its neighbors and so forth, Johnston reminds us that, as the *bingjia* or military writers understood, weapons are tools. His examination of China's military actions since 1949 indicates that, consistent with realist theory, China's resort to force has 'been related to improved relative capabilities' while when in a crisis, China tends to act in a more conflictual manner as it grew relatively stronger."[25]

An ironic aspect of this hundred-year fencing match, which is now on an even footing, is that during this process, the West has slowly moved toward the original Chinese position of inequality. This is not official international relations doctrine; the great step was taken, however, in the ratification of the UN Charter, when the extant states agreed that there would be five permanent members of the Security Council, each with a veto vote, while the rest of the membership would occupy a lesser status. This is a matter, we shall see in Chapter 8, of continuing agitation to those who feel left out of the action and demeaned by the two-tier status. In brief, the reality of power is more clearly evident in this arrangement, and deliberately so. The implications of this situation and the Chinese hierarchical experience will be considered later on.

25. Ibid., 38.

5   Historicism and Progress: Transcending Human Nature?

Thus far, our study has established the historical realist position through empirical examples in a variety of geographical areas. We have demonstrated the rationale of the state in preserving itself and functioning as an actor in interstate relations from Thucydides through Machiavelli. The philosophy of interest, power, and morality as a goal for state action was sufficient to the day. Machiavelli's complaint about politics, about the political system per se, was not that it was either good or bad, but rather that no one had appeared in Italy in his time who had sufficiently mastered the technique of power to create a united Italian state. The purpose of that enterprise was to recapture the glory of Rome.

So far we have seen that as the centuries advanced, the perduring character of human nature held firm against the occasional idealistic aspirations of the Abbé de Saint Pierre for peaceful solutions to conflicts between nations, calling upon Christian religious principles of love and forgiveness. Human nature would shift from the Old to the New Testament. By the time of Augustine (A.D. 354–450), the Church, grounded as it was in the fallibility of man, gave up on eliminating war altogether and opted for the principles of the "just war" for both prudential and religious reasons (see Chapter 6). Immanuel Kant, a deeply religious man, recognized that human nature seemed to prefer conflict to cooperation and decided to look in another direction to see if a basis for peace could be located. He thought there was a possibility of curbing mankind and its lust for war through a significant institutional change, that is, to rid the world of monarchy, which welcomed war, and to create a world of republics that would welcome peace. *Perpetual Peace,* which we have explored in detail, was his answer to this dilemma (see Chapter 3).

Across the globe, the Chinese Empire created what amounted to the later French concept of a *cordon sanitaire,* a belt of vassal states or satrapies all along its vast borders that allowed China to keep its adversaries at arm's length. The aim of this empire was to exercise its power through its superior culture, backed up by superior force, the one validating the other. It looked upon change as chaos and preferred stability to progress.[1] With these objectives, it is no wonder that the inventions already known to the court—gunpowder, navigational aids, and so on—were neglected and that later, the West used similar knowledge to launch the Industrial Revolution and to create modern military forces.[2] The lesson for the Chinese was not that they should change their traditional values; on the contrary, they would henceforth tack on Western technology but keep their traditional philosophy, not understanding the impossibility of this approach, that is, the relationship between economics and sociology. They wanted to meet Western force with Western-style force, but without their own technological base. Only recently have the Chinese put these ideas together. The political utility of the old tributary idea has not been abandoned, as the culture again becomes strong, and Chinese international relations, based on hierarchical power, begin to shape the twenty-first century. Power based on culture, national identity, and military might is a familiar Chinese tradition.[3] All of the above can be accommodated in the context of historical realism.

The attempts to break entirely from historical realism, that is, the limiting factor of human nature and its motivations, rose to their apex in the nineteenth and twentieth centuries. As I have just discussed, Kant with his call for a world of republics was a forerunner of this idea; during the whole of the nineteenth century, however, there was no rush on the part of the monarchies to eliminate themselves and no one else was able to change many of the forms of government. The French Revolution, which Kant saw as promising, was soon negated in form, at least, by the rise of Napoleon and his creation of a new monarchy. His exploitation of French nationalism almost allowed him to accomplish his imperial aims, only to fail in Russia. The counterrevolution then began in full force and the day of the republic would have to await the conclusion of World War I.

In addition to Kant and his republic, three other philosophical tendencies

1. See Herbert Butterfield, Cho Yunhsu, and William McNeil, "On Chinese and World History," conference at Hong Kong University, 1970.

2. See Lester C. Thurow, *The Future of Capitalism: How Today's Economic Forces Shape Tomorrow's Future* (New York: Basic Books, 1996).

3. See Johnston, *Cultural Reason*, and also an essay on China's economy, politics, and culture: Wang Gungwu, *The Chinese Way: China's Position in International Relations* (Oslo: Scandinavian University Press, 1995).

arose to challenge the basic tenets of realism. The first two were the philosophy of Georg F. W. Hegel (1770–1831), based on freedom and democracy and explicated by Hegel's historicism grounded in the dialectic, and that of Karl Marx (1815–1883), who reinterpreted the world as a history of economics, in that each era—feudal, capitalist, socialist-communist—in turn produced its own unique economic system. Each such system created its own superstructure of culture, politics, and society. This development proceeded by the dialectic formula— thesis, antithesis, synthesis—finally eliminating class antagonisms and ending in a classless, communist society. Then came the slogan, "To each according to his needs; from each according to his ability." Remnants of this formula for unending social strife still operate in the old Soviet empire.

The third antagonist of historical realism, also a version of historicism, was Progress. The concept did not derive from a single individual but is rather a way of looking at the world. It probably can be formally grounded in the Enlightenment, beginning with the French in the eighteenth century and taken up by the British and Scots. Based on the progress of the sciences, Condorcet, Comte, and later Darwin and Spencer and many others thought these same techniques would result in a new "social science" that would bring about the perfectibility of man. This of course was totally contrary to the realist and religious tradition. Each of these three challenges will be discussed in more detail.

The issue that attracted Hegel was freedom, arising as it did from the event and then the failure of the French Revolution. It was clear that the "rights of man" could be brutally abused and that the guarantee of freedom had to come from another direction. (None of this, however, in any way diminished Hegel's admiration for Napoleon as the embodiment of the world spirit and as a victim of petty critics, the fleas and lice of the body politic.) The ongoing influence of the Enlightenment also cast its shadow over the study of the social sciences and philosophy and religion. There was an obsession with what was nature and what were its laws. If everyone behaved according to natural laws, then man was not free and never would be. The Germans, interested as always in vast universal explanations, also wondered about the permanence of human nature, whether it could account for so many variations of civilizations; but on the whole, this was not the center of their attack. How was nature related to human freedom? It was finally here that Hegel proposed an answer: the dialectic.

The dialectic indeed is an old device, dating back to Plato. In the early nineteenth century, Greek culture was brought to the fore (perhaps reconstructed) in Germany by Friedrich Schiller, Hegel's friend and an art critic, who much admired classical Greek art and poetry. Hegel wanted to know how a similar high standard of art could be constructed for Germany, recognizing that the language and ideas would not be accessible to the whole society (although he realized that had been true in Greece as well). These dilemmas had to be resolved, just as the master problem of nature and freedom needed to be settled, if his philosophy was to mature. The blending of the laws of nature and natural development with the idea of the free will would be accomplished by the old Platonic device: the collision of opposites to create a new and higher level of resolution. The real destiny of free will was with nature, and the natural outcome of man's quest was freedom in democracy.

Hegel was keen on making sense out of history. He began with the origin of the slave-master relationship and how the world passed through three stages of freedom: the time of the Oriental despot, where only one man was free; the classical states of antiquity, where some were free and the rest slaves; and the modern German liberal state, where everyone was free. This was the dialectic machine of history, with irresistible democratic states everywhere, realizing its full potential for freedom.

Hegel also had an important place in his philosophy for morality. He believed that morality can create a will that wills both private and universal principles of right. It follows that freedom can be similarly willed and become part of nature, the outcome of the process of nature itself. With nature as the thesis and freedom as the antithesis, the new and ever higher synthesis was an expanding area of freedom as the natural destiny of man, the outcome of his struggle for self-realization. The individual can accomplish this result only within the state. Like Aristotle, Hegel believed that only the state, capable of issuing laws for a good society, could enable the individual to maximize all of his good potential. Rehabilitating the moral position of the state, after the excesses of the French Revolution, was one of Hegel's purposes. Contrary to Kant, Hegel believed that the supremacy and autonomy of the state allowed it to consider whatever measures it deemed necessary to promote its own interests, including war. This position placed Hegel in the twentieth-century realist camp at the same time that his dialectic kept him outside.

In his posthumously published *Philosophy of History*, Hegel wrote about the progression of freedom through history in the three stages listed above. The spirit of freedom would realize itself in successive states; at the end of his life, Hegel thought the world spirit was in East Prussia, but it was bound to go on from place to place, where conditions were the ripest to maximize freedom. This was man's deserved fate.

One notes that the "world spirit" was not the product of any one nation or culture but moved about as required by the objective conditions of the state. Hegel was certain that it had settled down in Napoleon and the French nation and was unstinting in his praise of Napoleon, particularly after seeing the emperor, astride his horse, at Jena, Prussia, in 1806. Napoleon's decline and downfall filled Hegel with chagrin, but nothing could be done to save Napoleon; the world spirit moved on, this time to Germany. Hegel's subsequent philosophy was dedicated to what that meant and how his own historiography, dictated by the ineluctable march of the dialectic, would track the evolution of freedom and democracy in the world.

For some decades (before the recent comeback of his work through Francis Fukuyama), Hegel dropped out of the popular culture. His interpretation of history was out of vogue. In part this was because the world spirit idea was not self-evident. Where was it going next, and what was it going to do? Then Hegel was overtaken by another dialectician, Karl Marx, who used the same process, except applying it foremost to the economic world, not the political and spiritual, to account for history in a new way that had startling consequences.

In 1848 *The Communist Manifesto,* written by Friedrich Engels (Marx's collaborator and financial supporter) and Marx, burst on the European scene. "A specter is haunting Europe, the specter of Communism," began the pamphlet. "All the powers of old Europe have entered into a holy alliance to exorcise this specter. Pope and Czar. Metternich and Guizot, French radicals and German police spies."[4] Here was the whole theory of how the world worked, a product of economic interaction. This theory explained imperialism in clear economic terms, how the world progressed from feudalism to capitalism, and then why it dialectically would finally rise to socialism and then communism.

Marx's ideas on the deficiencies of capitalism appeared in his later volumes of *Das Capital,* including the "surplus value" idea that because labor added more value to a product than capital, the capitalist unfairly pocketed that value which belonged to labor. And so on. The excesses of the Industrial Revolution were appearing, especially in England, the first of the new industrialized nations; socialism, the control of the economy by the state, was becoming an acceptable idea to counter the capitalist. The working class was large enough to support a political party with a chance of winning an election, or at least of achieving some power. Marx's description of how the imperial powers were forced to go abroad for raw materials and new markets to support the ever higher demands for production and sales, and how the manufactured goods overwhelmed handicraft workers and reduced them to poverty, contained enough truth to turn the minds of the common people. One reason for the at-

---

4. Karl Marx and Friedrich Engels, *The Communist Manifesto* (Northbrook, Ill.: AHMM Publishing Corporation, 1955), 8.

traction of these ideas as being practical was that they had not yet been put into play in a real government.[5]

The real test of Marx's thesis did not come to pass, however, until the Russian Revolution of 1917. It is not my purpose to go through the ups and downs of that affair—the failure of the Kerensky democratic government and the rise of the Bolsheviks under Lenin, who finally established a socialist state. But once again the state seemed to be on the verge of failure because it tried to go against the principles of realism, that is, it did not adequately deal with the human characteristics of interest, lust for power, and morality and thus did not conduct the revolution in a practical way. The Paris commune in the previous century had similarly failed, so Lenin was now faced with what was to be done. In his classic *State and Revolution*, Lenin decided he could carry the revolution to a successful conclusion by adding the missing power element, namely, mass leadership, the vanguard of the proletariat, or the Communist Party. Without such an organization to anticipate the wishes and goals of the proletariat, the revolution would become diffuse and go nowhere. Such was the genius of Lenin, yet as it turned out, by 1989 this formulation proved to be in practice grossly inadequate. The Communist Party in Russia and elsewhere was driven out of power by the very people it claimed to lead, and new forces emerged to defeat the communists. Political loss, however, is seldom a permanent condition, even in Greek days; personalities and parties came and went, each determined to establish a permanent coalition and power base, but always to be frustrated by new conditions that no amount of political crystal gazing, or any number of rational choice models, could foretell.

It is fair to say that the first two challengers to historical realism were ultimately not successful. Both Hegelian and Marxian philosophy started out with high promise, but both failed in their principal objective, namely, providing humanity with a blueprint for political, economic, and social progress. But this was not known as they began their historic journey from the mid-nineteenth century to the present. These two philosophies were in fact overshadowed by a far greater and better-known phenomenon, of which they were a cultural part, the idea of Progress. Progress with a capital "P" was a more virulent strain of small-letter "progress," which exists as an empirical fact in everyday life in a variety of fields, especially those concerned with science and technology. Progress was seen by the cognoscenti as the natural order of things. It was and is another form of historicism but not dependent on the dialectic idea.

---

5. For the vicissitudes of socialism in the present century, see Robert J. Myers, "The Crises of Socialism," *Society*, November–December 1995, 27–31.

Even if the world spirit did not arrive in France until the time of Napoleon, according to Hegel, Progress seemed to center in Paris in the eighteenth century, when an extraordinary group of scholars and savants somehow accumulated there and, seemingly without design, created the French Enlightenment. An account of this phenomenon of Progress was recorded in 1920 in a book by J. B. Bury of Cambridge and then reprinted with an introduction by Charles Beard as part of the Century of Progress Exposition held in Chicago in the early 1930s.[6] Such was the hold that Progress had on the popular imagination.

Beard in his introduction amplifies some of the themes I have touched on before, particularly the Greek idea of an ongoing disintegration in the world as well as Saint Augustine's conviction that the Christian era was the final chapter of life on earth. These ideas were profoundly against the possibility of a countertrend in society, namely, the proposition of progress. In fact, as the Dark Ages advanced, so did the preoccupation with the past. As Bury noted, "With the loss of freedom pessimism increased, and the Greek philosophies of resignation were needed more than ever. Those whom they could not satisfy turned their thoughts to new mystical philosophies and religions, which were little interested in the earthly destinies of human society."[7]

And Beard says about the Christian position: "For Augustine, as for the medieval believer, the course of history would be satisfactorily complete if the world came to an end in his own lifetime. He was not interested in the question whether any gradual amelioration of society or increase in knowledge would mark the period of time which still remain[ed] to run before the Day of Judgment. In Augustine's system the Christian era introduced the last period of history, the old age of humanity, which would endure only so long as to enable the Deity to gather in the predestined number of saved people." This theory might be combined with the widespread belief in a millennium on earth, but the conception of such a dispensation does not render it a theory of Progress.[8]

The crises of the Christian church came about in part because of the delay in the second coming of Christ. The New Testament abounds in expectation that the end of the world is at hand; this created a Jimmy Carter–like malaise: why exert oneself or plan ahead if the miracle was almost upon us? The condition in the early days of Christianity is caught in Elaine Pagels's *Gnostic Gospels*.[9] Fur-

---

6. J. B. Bury, *The Idea of Progress: An Inquiry into Its Origin and Growth*, 1920 (New York: Dover, 1987).

7. Ibid., 20.

8. Ibid.

9. Elaine Pagels, *The Gnostic Gospels* (New York: Vantage Books, 1989).

ther, the gradual collapse of the Roman Empire placed the new religion in jeopardy; was the sack of Rome caused by people turning away from the old and familiar pagan gods in favor of Jesus Christ? This accusation caused much agitation among church leaders. Augustine, a convert to Christianity later in life, responded with *The City of God* to reassure the faithful of the correctness of their choice. (There was a powerful urge in the early Christian era to harmonize Hellenic and Christian belief.) As Werner Jaeger wrote, "The dream of Alexander when he founded the city that bears his name was now to be realized: two universal systems, Greek culture and the Christian church, were to be united in the mighty superstructure of Alexandrian theology."[10] In Augustine's time, attention was given not to progress and reconciliation with the future but rather to the glories of the past. No modern man could expect to approach the epoch of the classical Greeks, whose poets and writers, like Homer, would never know an equal. Yet even among Augustine's followers, a monk from Portugal began noting the exceptional number of advances in simple technology occurring in the daily lives of the people. Waiting for the Apocalypse, with eyes turned upward, the Church had missed the achievements of the folk on earth. Finally, it became apparent that the only explanation for these events was that the Apocalypse, comprising the end of the earth and the bodily ascension to Heaven, had been postponed. The Book of Revelation was scrutinized again and again, and though the ultimate end was not in question, the timing was.

Turning from the religious critique of progress, we look into J. B. Bury's treatise on the idea of Progress. Bury begins with a discussion of the two kinds of ideas he finds before him, those that are considered good or bad, related to human aims and determined by will, such as liberty, toleration, and equality of opportunity; and those that are considered either true or false, including metaphysical ideas. Progress is one of the ideas that is considered to be true and recognized in all societies. Nonetheless, there remains a variety of interpretations as to just what this means and what parameters ought to apply to politics, for example. Once again, we will need to consider one of the articles of faith of historical realism, that is, the immutable character of human nature, as it faces the challenge of Progress.

The question of whether Progress is embedded in nature and automatically will carry all before it is of no small matter; if that is so, then human nature will be hard to exclude from its purview. Certainly we see change in the physical and social world about us, but this does not necessarily mean that human nature

---

10. Werner Jaeger, *Early Christianity and Greek Paideia* (Cambridge, Mass.: Belknap Press of Harvard University Press, 1961), 40.

changes; that would be true only if there were a natural law that is part of an inevitable idea of how the world works with human nature necessarily caught up in this upward progression. This is the position that Herbert Spencer took in trying to develop his "Synthetic Philosophy," which was to be the complete explanation of God's (or the Unknowable's) plan for the earth; this theory was slowly revealing itself to Spencer, spurred on by Darwin's evolutionary discoveries. As Bury put it, "By the simultaneous advances of geology and biology man's perspective in time was revolutionized, just as the Copernican astronomy had revolutionized his perspective in space. Many thoughtful and many thoughtless people were ready to discern—as Huxley suggested—in man's long progress through the past, a reasonable ground of faith in his attainment of a nobler future."[11]

Briefly, there were two principal objections that began to arise to dampen the optimism that greeted Spencer's optimistic work. First, this idea of Progress meant that children would presumably inherit favorable characteristics of intelligence and artistic ability from their parents, for example, in a version of Lamarckian biological progress, which would then mean that each generation would be on the road to perfection. But this did not happen in real life. Some children were inferior to their parents. Second, as in the case of children, some civilizations attained a certain growth and accumulation of modernity only to falter and then disintegrate. For this reason, some contemporary philosophers, like the German Rudolf Lotze, asserted emphatically in 1864 that people were not on the path to perfection, that "human nature will not change."[12]

Lotze wrote: "Never one fold and one shepherd, never one uniform culture for all mankind, never universal noblesse. Our virtue and happiness can only flourish amid an active conflict with wrong. If every stumbling block were smote away, men would no longer be like man but like a flock of innocent brutes, feeding on good things provided by nature as at the very beginning of their course."[13]

Some of the arguments on the question of human nature arise from the differences in human temperament. Evolution, Bury says, can lead to a "pessimistic as well as to an optimistic interpretation."[14] In eras of prosperity and good feeling, naturally people look positively on events and their prospects; whereas in times of discontent and hardship, an opposite view is more likely to prevail.

11. Bury, *Idea of Progress*, 342.
12. Ibid, 343.
13. Quoted ibid., 341.
14. Ibid., 345.

Martin Wight deals with attitude and temperament for his three categories of international relations theory—realists, rationalists, and revolutionaries. The realists, he says, are pessimistic about human nature, expecting aggressive behavior and self-interest and conflict to dominate. Wight cites the usual historical figures—Machiavelli, Hobbes, Bismarck. He also concludes with what he calls the "Hobbesian paradox," that if one wishes to escape from the war of "every man against every man," then "the social contract may throw up a tyrant worse than the state of nature."[15]

Wight's "revolutionists" tend to be optimistic and perfectionistic about human nature. There is again a paradox, this time after Rousseau, "Man is born free, but everywhere he is in chains." This implies that a band of evildoers is at work. If such people could somehow be eliminated, the world would be better. The Soviet class struggle was calculated to achieve those results, leaving in its wake a better citizen. The French Revolution, through its "depopulation program," hoped to achieve a "virtuous residue."

Wight's additional category of theorists, the "rationalists," were neither optimistic nor pessimistic, relying on reason alone. For them society is "largely a successful field of cooperation between rational persons. The Rationalist therefore is a reformist, the practitioner of piecemeal social engineering." Rationalists are tied to the linear progress of history, culminating in success, while realists look at the world as unending cyclical progression. As for Progress, Wight said it was "written large and plain on the pages of history, but progress is not a law of nature. The ground gained by one generation may be lost by the next. The thoughts of men may flow into the channels which lead to disaster and barbarism."[16] As for human nature, the question of attitude or outlook does not affect the argument, dealt with at the outset of this book, about its apparent immutability over known historical time.

Bury, acknowledging the great contribution to the age of scientific discoveries and emancipation from superstitions and the past in general made by the rationalists and their promotion of Progress, nonetheless does not believe that Progress is a law of nature. Many prominent persons (and many more not so prominent, Bury says) failed in the effort to prove it so. Overlooked in their desire to establish Progress as a law was what Bury calls "the illusion of finality": "If we accept the reasoning upon which the dogma of Progress is based, must we not carry them to their full conclusion? . . . In other words, does not Progress itself suggest that its value as a doctrine is only relative, corresponding to a

---

15. Wight, *International Theory*, 25–26.
16. Ibid., 25–29.

certain not very advanced stage of civilization; just as Providence, in its day, was an idea of relative value, corresponding to a stage somewhat less advanced? Can it be said that this argument is merely a disconcerting trick of dialectic played under cover of the darkness in which the issue of the future is safely hidden by Horde's prudent god?"[17]

This discourse seems to settle the fate of Progress; it comes and goes and is not inevitable. So its challenge to historical realism and the constancy of human nature is only contingent. The other two doctrines, those of Hegel and Marx, have run up against their severest critic, Sir Karl Popper, who equally disputed those who believed in the laws of history, laws of social development, or laws of Progress. He saw no proof of any foreordained direction of history and demonstrated to his (and many other people's) satisfaction the correctness of his analysis in *The Poverty of Historicism*.[18]

Popper's dedication gives the tenor of the book: "In memory of the countless men, women, and children of all creeds or nations or races who fell victim to the fascist and communist belief in Inexorable Laws of Historical Destiny." The preface says that "for strictly logical reasons, it is impossible for us to predict the future course of history."[19] Popper was preoccupied with this issue against the background of the claims of fascism and communism. All of us have had the opportunity to witness this in the collapse of the Soviet Union and its communist ideology. In this crisis, both the former Soviet leaders and the West, led by the United States, demonstrated the continuity of historical realism as the pragmatic base of international relations. The arguments from power and interest and moral claims on both sides so far have kept the peace and reigned over a difficult transition of the world order. This is no small accomplishment and recommendation for realism and its philosophy, which has stood the test of time and challenges, sometimes bizarre and always fraught with danger.

The empirical facts so far suggest that the realist tradition will continue, which means that idealism will still be a prod for hope and change, a new evolution, but that the old problems of international relations are likely to remain intact—especially the issues of war and peace, which provide the yeast for the bread of politics. We will next consider how realism tries to deal with war, under the rubric of "just war," and how that plays out in the contemporary scene. Realism still stays with its triad of interest, power, and morality. Kant, as we have seen, is ready to concede those points but is convinced that war can be

---

17. Bury, *Idea of Progress*, 352.
18. Karl Popper, *The Poverty of Historicism* (New York: Routledge, 1991).
19. Ibid., 6.

abated if not eliminated (he does not exclude that possibility); he puts his faith not in the flawed nature of mankind but rather in the possibility of creating a political system based on the idea of republicanism that will, in a flick of the administrative wand, simply make war impossible. Kant's legacy has continued to exert a powerful appeal into this century in such institutions as the United Nations, where administrative forms and rules are supposed to do the job Kant strove for. (To be sure, Kant had no idea how an international bureaucracy would operate. It would require the arrival of Max Weber at the turn of the twentieth century to alert us to this phenomenon.)

Finally, all this will show the law of unintended consequences in full operation, that striving for the good does not necessarily make it so, and that the reverse side of applications in the real world shows up not in some idealized world but rather in creating precedents that further compound and complicate the problem being faced.

6   Alternative to Peace: The Just War

The critics and opponents of realism charge that its proponents accept the recurrence of war in international (and domestic) politics as growing out of human nature, the struggle for power, and the need for a moral guide to policy. This indeed is correct. It is important to understand this issue in terms of the contemporary argument. Idealists such as Erasmus and the Abbé Saint Pierre would abolish warfare altogether. Basically they would improve human nature to a point where a new man would arise intent only on peaceful purposes. Historicism in its Hegelian, Marxian, or progressive modes would eliminate war through the establishment of new kinds of societies. And so would Kant with his league of republics.

The premises of the doctrine of realism do not lead to pacifism in the face of challenge, nor do they anticipate the elimination of war as an instrument of state power. This philosophy anticipates that skilled statesmen, following their understanding of their nation's interest, the power available to them (and their allies), and their vision of a moral end of politics, will limit the occasions when war is the only option. Realists favor the building of institutions—democracies or even international cooperative bodies such as the UN—as a way of perhaps lessening the prospects for war, but they are under no illusion that these institutions alone will eliminate war altogether. This is a fair representation of how U.S. foreign policy is strategically conducted.

These expectations are rooted in realism's ultimate conception of the flawed nature of humankind; like the Christian religion, it does not make claims for the perfectibility of man in historic time. Therefore, the best that can be done for now is to limit the occasions for war through skilled application of diplomacy and placing opprobrium on aggression. This stance positions realism in concert with the just war doctrine as it was originally associated with Saint Augustine and Thomas Aquinas (1225–1274), leading figures in the Catholic

Church's efforts, beginning with the fall of the law-and-order Roman Empire, to save civilization from total plunder. As will be explained, the reasons for the just war approach were complex. And realism has willy-nilly subscribed to some version of just war theory for as long as has the Catholic Church. Whether the concept of the just war should be part of the realist position in the future is one of the concerns of this discussion.

It is generally accepted that the revival of American interest in the traditional concept of the just war began sometime during the undeclared war in Vietnam. Some might mark it with the publication of Michael Walzer's *Just and Unjust Wars.* Walzer's motivation is spelled out in part in his introduction to the original edition of the book. He first deprecates the international law fraternity and its emphasis on "positive law" for an international community that does not exist. Then he explains his own purpose: "I want to recapture the just war for political and moral theory. My own work, then, looks back to the religious tradition within which Western politics and morality were first given shape, to the books of virtues like Maimonides, Aquinas, Vitoria, and Suarez—and then to the books written by Hugo Grotius, who took over the tradition and began to work it into secular form. But I have not attempted a history of just war theory, and I quote the classical texts only occasionally for the sake of some particularly illuminating or forceful argument. I refer more often to contemporary philosophers and theologians (and soldiers and statesmen) for my main concern is not with the making of the moral world but with its present character."[1]

Later in his career, Walzer seized the opportunity created by the Persian Gulf War in 1991 to write a new preface and issue a second edition in 1992. Now perhaps he is more skeptical of the whole enterprise: "This is a dangerous moment for any theory, though it is also, obviously, a moment to which theorists look forward. Think of the perverse, if exhilarating effects upon religion whenever the language of holiness is taken over by politicians. Of course, politics and war are never holy—not, at least, as I understand holiness—while they are sometimes, or to some degree, just. But only some times and to some degree, and when more blanket justifications are claimed, the theory is rendered suspect. If it can be used to defend injustice, should it be used at all?"[2]

In this chapter I will reflect on whether the good that the just war theory intends actually outweighs the evil that a doctrine so available to self-interested interpretation allows. Hans J. Morgenthau poses this problem for nation-states:

---

1. Michael Walzer, *Just and Unjust Wars: A Moral Argument with Historical Illustrations* (New York: Basic Books, 1977), xxviii.

2. Walzer, *Just and Unjust Wars,* 2d ed. (New York: Basic Books, 1992), xi.

"There is a world of difference between the belief that all nations stand under the judgment of God, inscrutable in the human mind, and the blasphemous conviction that God is always on one's side and that what one wills oneself cannot fail to be willed by God also."[3]

For this writer, as for Walzer, it was the Vietnam War that challenged the just war theory—not the utility of the theory but its legitimacy, which is another question altogether. States need to promote war to their citizens as just or right to ensure participation and public support, but this may have little to do with justice, assuming that an objective standard of justice is available. Contemporary "just warriors" often simply note the criteria (which will be listed shortly) and assume that their own country passes the test. The built-in relativity is ignored. Universal justice requires something more: it can reside in the perfection of a particular religion, a Kantian imperative, a belief in utilitarianism, or a short list of virtues so that there is no blinking at the right or wrong of a matter. Yet even for religion the tests are severe, as was brought home in the American Civil War. To many, the question of which side God was on was entirely legitimate, although offers made by earnest religious leaders to intercede with him on President Abraham Lincoln's behalf were gently turned down. If God wished to advise Lincoln, there was nothing standing in the way.

The operational justice of everyday life, however, when it comes to matters of war and peace, is apt to be both chauvinistic and nationalistic, thereby in the case of America leading to moralistic approaches to those matters. Certainly from the perspective of most Americans, the U.S. entry into World Wars I and II, the Korean "police action" under UN auspices, and the Gulf War in 1991 placed justice on the side of America and its allies. For many, Vietnam was an anomaly, although claims about justice are still debated. As a degree of relativism is necessary in considering the justice of war, it is not surprising that this justice remains a matter of both heated and learned controversy.

Some associate the beginning of the just war tradition with Augustine, although he was no enthusiast; even the just war, he said, is a "cruel necessity," and even if the aggressor meets his due, "[war] is a trouble and misfortune."[4] Later Catholic canonists and a rich collection of jurists such as Hugo Grotius, Jean Bodin, Alberto Gentile, and others in the sixteenth century codified the rules of the just war. The international lawyers, however, were less concerned with justice (even though just war language entered into international law) than with the intricacies of international law, which gave each sovereign state an

---

3. Morgenthau, *Politics among Nations,* 3d ed., 11.
4. See Ernest Barker, *Essays on Government,* 2d ed. (Oxford: Clarendon Press, 1951), 248.

"equal right" to go to war. This shift in concern brought about the temporary eclipse of the just war theory, and the concept was revived only after World War II, a war that needed, in the eyes of most of humankind, no justification beyond good triumphant over evil. (One leaves aside here important means arguments over firebombings and the atomic bombings of Japan.)

Robert Tucker has expressed concern about nuclear deterrence and the temptation for one side or another to break it under the guise of a "defensive" first strike. He was skeptical about moralism and the possibility of an aggressor (even an American!) launching such a war. It may be, Tucker writes, "that what men conceive to be their interests and, consequently, the actions they take, will eventually be influenced by claims whose roots are found in [the] need for self-justification."[5] Paul Ramsey addressed the nuclear question as a Christian theologian, trying to justify a "limited nuclear" war, but in the end his treatment brought no greater moral weight to bear on the nuclear dilemma than did the more recent labors of the Catholic bishops, with their agonized conclusion that nuclear weapons and threats were immoral, but what is a poor bishop to do?[6] The growing moral issue of Vietnam and the messiness of the American conscience prepared the background for Walzer's book.

Now that the broad brushstrokes are behind us, what are some of the specifics of a just war scenario? There is little argument about the criteria, which are expressed in the following, taken from Robert Phillips. There are two principal categories in the just war tradition, *jus ad bellum* (steps leading up to war) and *jus in bello* (the rules of engagement, so to speak). In *jus ad bellum*, the steps must be a last resort, declared by legitimate authority, and morally justifiable. Morally justifiable actions include self-defense against aggression, correction of an injustice that has gone uncorrected by legitimate authority "in another place," reestablishment of a social order that will distribute justice, and action undertaken with the intention of bringing about peace. (All of these ideas apply equally to the concept of "intervention," which nowadays is a much more frequent occurrence than declared war. See Chapter 8.) Then, if the issue is not yet settled, we move into *jus in bello*. Here we have two principles: "(1) proportionality: The quantity of force employed or threatened must always be morally proportionate to the end being sought in war; and (2) discrimination: Force

---

5. Robert W. Tucker, *The Just War: A Study in Contemporary American Doctrine* (Baltimore: Johns Hopkins University Press, 1960), 4.

6. Paul Ramsey, *The Just War: Force and Political Responsibility* (New York: Charles A. Scribner's, 1968). For a complete treatment of this important issue, see his "Challenge of Peace: God's Promise and Our Response," *Origins*, 19 May 1983, 1–32.

must never be applied in such a way as to make noncombatants and innocent persons the intentional objects of attack. The only appropriate targets in war are combatants." Under these circumstances, one must call upon the principle of double effect: "In a situation where the use of force can be foreseen to have actual or probable multiple effects, some of which are evil, culpability does not attach to the agent if the following conditions are met: (a) the action must carry the intention to produce morally good consequences; (b) the evil effects are not intended as ends in themselves or as means to other ends, good or evil; (c) the permission of collateral evil must be justified by considerations of proportionate moral weight."[7]

If this argument has the lugubrious sound of medieval scholasticism, then we are on track to understanding where this collection of rules of war originated: in the monasteries of the Catholic Church as it tried to restore civic and social order to the collapsing Roman Empire. Order was more important than justice in those parlous times. But justice is surely not the principal motivator of war (correcting an injustice is one of the minor rights of the just war concept but potentially very troublesome). As I have already noted, Donald Kagan, in his book *On the Origins of War*, quotes with approval Thucydides, who found that people go to war out of "honor, fear, and interest." If these are the three causes, how, then, do we get into the idea of justice in war? We want to know that "right" is on our side, yet I will argue later that right is obviously not the same as justice. Tucker in his critical study of just war theory says that "historically, states interpreted the principle of justice in war in such an elastic way that they have caused them to seem compatible with any act of war." This observation is the source of my uneasiness in reading about just war theory in such standard texts as Walzer and also James Turner Johnson's *Can Modern War Be Just?* and *Just War Tradition and the Restraint of War*, as well as seeing the daily bloody display reported in the media.[8]

Note that there is no expectation in just war theory of removing war altogether from international society. For realists, that at least is a positive factor. Kagan has no such expectation either; he quotes Heraclitus, who says, "War is the father of all things." The goal of just war theory, then, is to limit the frequency of war and to burden conduct with moral opprobrium when just war

7. Robert L. Phillips, *War and Justice* (Norman: University of Oklahoma Press, 1984), 12–13. Also see John Temple Swing, ed., *Right v. Might* (New York: Council on Foreign Relations, 1991).

8. Tucker, *Just War*, 15; James Turner Johnson, *Can Modern War Be Just?* (New Haven: Yale University Press, 1984), and *Just War Tradition and the Restraint of War: A Moral and Historical Inquiry* (Princeton: Princeton University Press, 1981).

rules are not followed. But why would anyone follow rules that interfere with victory and retribution, which often figure in the way enemies, old and new, pursue their aims once they have crossed the dangerous Rubicon of war? Can we—should we—judge the justice of wars on the basis of an unsound, perhaps immoral theory?

The Catholic Church's involvement with the just war doctrine in the fifth century is explained by Robert Phillips in *War and Justice.* Phillips discusses the Church's role in avoiding the proliferation of armed conflict: "The first line of response is theological. *Bellum Justum* in its traditional form is one important aspect of medieval political theory which receives its clearest expression in the Augustinian contrast between the *City of God* and the *City of Man.* In that context statecraft will also be seen as an essentially imperfect means for the distribution of justice. This state will have its necessities, but they will be subordinate to a higher law."[9] This point, of course, was essential to the Church, if in addition to participating in the councils of kings and princes, it was going to maintain its claim of access to divine judgment.

It also meant, as Phillips interestingly explains, that the Church in this instance turned its back on Christ and the New Testament, and thus on Christianity. The New Testament was pacifist—in it we have the turning of the other check and love, not war—and pacifism put the Christians in opposition to the state. Phillips cites cases, including the tragedy of a Roman youth, Maximillan, who said, "I cannot enlist [in the Roman army] for I am a Christian." This assertion cost him his head.

Phillips also recounts the early Christians' belief in the imminent return of Christ (a belief that any fair reading of the New Testament would substantiate). Thus, according to Phillips, "the moral admonitions against violence expressed by Jesus are inextricably mixed with passivity—a serene waiting in faith for the end of the world."[10] Importantly, this attitude of waiting for the world to end had some unintended consequences: it discouraged all future-oriented economic activity. Everything was predictably worse—the golden age, the silver age, the bronze age. Life operated in cycles, the past always superior to the present and the future inferior to what now existed. Elaine Pagels in *The Origin of the Devil* reports on wrongs not righted in the early Christian community because of the belief in the imminent end of the world. Finally, someone looked around and saw there were many new and good inventions and much knowl-

9. Phillips, *War and Justice*, 13.
10. Ibid., 4–6.

edge that had accumulated since Christ's time and the predictions of the end of the world, and suddenly, in a historical sense, came the Enlightenment.

In the meantime, in the real world of the fifth century, Augustine was faced with the challenge of defending Christianity against its pagan attackers. The pagans claimed that it was because of Christianity that Rome turned its back on its reliable pantheon of gods and goddesses and that this was responsible for the sack of Rome in A.D. 410. To this challenge, Augustine responded with *The City of God*. He also strengthened his ties with the Roman powers that were. In brief, says Phillips, Augustine was willing to jettison at least some of Christ's teachings, which promoted pacifism, in favor of the "glory tales" of the Old Testament, God as the Lord of Battle. For Augustine, Christ's teachings became optional counsels of perfection or evangelical counsels. The Church would prefer to speak to the temporal power, and, with skill, prevail over it. All of this reveals the ubiquitous nature of the struggle for power. Augustine, educated as a Roman, had an inclusive attitude and used what he could of Greek, Roman, and Jewish wisdom.

In George H. Sabine's *History of Political Thought*, there is an outline of this struggle for power between church and state. The Church's idea was to cut off and claim the spiritual sphere and leave temporal matters to civil authorities while maintaining ultimate control over their decisions. The doctrine of "two swords" was enunciated by Pope Gelasius I at the end of the fifth century. To oil over differences that were (and still are) inherent in such a division and to ease the daily friction, a doctrine of "mutual helpfulness" was also promulgated. There was no doubt which side was superior. As Pope Gelasius said, "Christian emperors need bishops for the sake of eternal life, and bishops make use of imperial regulations to order the course of temporal affairs." One of the things the bishops "ordered" was the circumstances of the wars that plagued the Middle Ages. As Phillips writes, "Once the hurdle of pacifism had been surmounted, *bellum justum* developed almost naturally within the framework of medieval political philosophy."[11]

By following this condensed history, we can readily see why we have the term *just war* and why it often appears with quotation marks. Tucker's statement that any war was justified under such an elastic code cannot be the complete and final answer if we are genuinely seeking constraints on war-making and war-fighting—or peacekeeping and peacemaking, to use the current Orwellian terms. The religious attachment to the question of war, an attachment that

11. George H. Sabine, *A History of Political Theory* (New York: Henry Holt, 1950); Phillips, *War and Justice*, 9.

surely stems from conflicts of temporal interest, no matter how disguised, still persists. In fact, temporal authorities certain of ecclesiastical support welcome the seal of approval—as in Operation Just Cause in Panama in 1990. There almost always seems to be a perfect fit between church and state, as Walzer's earlier statement indicates.

The ongoing intensity of the struggle between church and state and its abiding importance in Europe over the past three hundred years is outlined in Pierre Manent's *Intellectual History of Liberalism*. From Manent's perspective, the church-state question has been and remains the dominant issue facing European politics. The just war is one area in which mutual benefits in the church and state have produced an unshakable alliance of interest. A state could declare war under any circumstances as a Machiavellian "necessity" and leave the matter there. In practice, however, as a way of ensuring domestic support and at least a modicum of international understanding and acquiescence, the state preferred to co-opt the moral authority of the Church. The Church, in turn, to keep its sword sharp, hustled in with piety and moral approval.

This argument demonstrates that the Church, in its ecclesiastic authority, had ruled that temporal matters were subject to its judgment. The state accepted that dictum for its own reasons, but at a cost to its power vis-à-vis the Church. To consider where first to aim our criticisms of the just war theory, it is important to understand that it is in fact the Church and not the state that sanctions war. The broader implications of this particular struggle for power are what make Manent's conclusion so striking.

Modern man, democratic man, says Manent, wants to free himself, recreate himself, but is caught in a seemingly irreducible dilemma. Nowhere can man as he now is or man's society and state escape the Church's judgment. Man establishes himself in nature and in the law, each of which is in conflict with the other. Man then tries to construct a body politic that transcends this separation. But this polity is still faced by its old adversary. Manent writes: "The Christian religion from which [the secular authorities of the seventeenth and eighteenth centuries] tried to protect the polity is just as weak today as civil society and the state. But even in its present weakness, that religion still leads us to seek a separation of nature and law that it once forced us to desire. *Vis a tergo* that pushed the nations of the West toward a society without religion, it still remains a sovereign in its apparent exhaustion, as if, in three centuries of 'accelerating' history, nothing had happened."[12]

---

12. Pierre Manent, *An Intellectual History of Liberalism,* trans. Rebecca Bolinski (Princeton: Princeton University Press, 1994), 117.

I have followed this church-state path only to demonstrate the perduring strength of moral and ethical input not from the sovereign state but rather from the ecclesiastical powers to which it acquiesces. This is the strength of the Church's critique, "speaking truth to power." And yet, this judgmental stance is no longer sufficient for the Christian right in America, for example. It now wishes to compete for power with the civil authority, rather than simply to stand in judgment.

For the moment, then, it is enough to emphasize that moral approval of war (and its first cousin intervention) is highly valued by the state and gives the solemn-faced clerics and their Pentagon acolytes their substantial influence over the rectitude of matters of war and peace. The Gulf War received little support in the United States as long as Secretary of State James Baker promoted it in terms of oil and jobs. Only in 1991, when President George Bush began using phrases like "moral and just," did the public respond, the United Nations coalesce, and Congress vote to support the war. At least one Pentagon official assured us that God was on our side. The Gulf War was a comparatively easy case, performed at a slow and measured rate, with clear stages, from Operation Desert Shield to Operation Desert Storm, and with time to pay attention to the rules of the game.

But what about the more difficult cases, such as Vietnam? There was a certain seamless quality about the defeat of the French at Dien Bien Phu in 1954 and the arrival of American advisers to replace them. That the French could not conquer the nationalist forces of Ho Chi-minh was a lesson lost. We can today turn to Robert S. McNamara's exceptional book *In Retrospect: The Tragedy and the Lessons of Vietnam* for singular insight into the most fateful and intense period of the war.[13] One's expectation was that McNamara's book would supply a self-serving apology for the "we were terribly wrong" syndrome. This was true in part. But this memoir contains insights into the idea of war as just. This is important because Americans historically have insisted on their preference for a just war—in fact, to participate in an unjust war was unthinkable. By 1961 a wider war seemed to be on the horizon when the entire Indochina region (the former French colonies of Laos, Cambodia, and Vietnam) crumbled as Dwight Eisenhower passed the baton to John F. Kennedy. The argument over U.S. intervention in Vietnam, however, was not posed in just war terms but rather in terms of international law. The United States had answered the call of a legitimate government to turn back invaders from the rival state of North Vietnam.

13. Robert S. McNamara, *In Retrospect: The Tragedy and Lessons of Vietnam* (New York: Random House, 1995).

Against this narrow legalistic argument there were few popular protests or warning statements from religious establishments. As McNamara points out repeatedly, this was the Cold War. Three strands of conventional wisdom were woven together to create an impenetrable blindfold for American leaders: the domino theory, that the fall of Vietnam would inexorably lead to the collapse of the whole of Indochina and Southeast Asia, and the United States might be forced to make a stand at the Thai border; the Sino-Soviet alliance was about to conquer the Third World through "wars of national liberation"; and a display of any weakness in Vietnam would undermine the United States' credibility with its NATO allies. With those three pillars of wisdom in place, self-imposed U.S. constraints severely limited both options and common sense; furthermore, Lyndon B. Johnson ascended to power and his policy was expressed in one word: win. (The theory that Kennedy would have pulled out before the escalations of 1964 and 1965 is part of the legend of Camelot.) McNamara had other complaints, including the lack of State Department expertise with regard to advice on Europe and the Soviet Union, a legacy of the McCarthy era, and insufficient coordination between military and diplomatic policies.

The key to understanding the Vietnam tragedy for McNamara and the United States, however, is recorded in a single paragraph of his book. In August 1967 there were congressional hearings on Vietnam yet again. The Pentagon's joint chiefs were ever "can do," believing they needed just a few hundred thousand more troops (five hundred thousand were already there). And McNamara would once again try to make his case for a limited war, which would gradually carry the day. Here is the critical information: "The day before [the hearings] began, the president warned me about the heat I would face. 'I am not worried about the heat, as long as I know what we are doing is right,' I told him. He looked at me without saying another word. Not surprisingly, the president's political antennae were more sensitive than mine."[14]

"As long as I know what we are doing is right." This is a statement right out of Kant, appropriate enough for a philosopher, one can suggest, but not for a secretary of defense. Not only was Johnson's political sense keener than McNamara's, but his sense of morality was more acute. So we have a situation in which the reasons for the intervention were faulty and the secretary of defense was fighting a crusade. The criterion was not strategy and success but "right." McNamara's statement accepts the validity of two dubious principles of Kantian philosophy: that reason is superior to experience and that principle is superior to consequences. One can elaborate at length on the dimensions of this

14. Ibid., 284.

folly. It required Richard Nixon and Henry Kissinger, after a decent interval, to look the facts of power in the eye and get out. In my view, the Vietnam War on balance failed the test of the just war criteria but not the Machiavellian test of necessity, given the circumstances of the day. Realism needs to make such distinctions.

I will now list some of my objections to the facile use and abuse of the term *just war* and the uncontested acceptance of its validity as our international and national moral standard. As the phrase now stands, we are corrupting the word *justice,* one of the four Great Virtues; in effect, just war theory is an ideological Band-Aid to cover the wounds on the body of Justice; we are also confusing "right" with "just," as McNamara did. "Right" can mean what is good for you and for your interest. It can be identical to might, and indeed "might is right" is a common identification. *Just,* on the other hand, means philosophically guaranteeing that all of the involved parties in a certain action get their due. For me, *right* is an aggressive word, ego-oriented and self-serving, as shown in the McNamara example and in the word's frequent use in daily life. *Just* puts itself in the spotlight of general approval and even universal acclaim.

In the end, the availability of this set of historical principles allows for an ease of manipulation that makes all wars just in the eyes of each set of participants. These principles, then, actually have no meaning, and there are no boundaries to the way in which they can be manipulated.

This leads to my penultimate observation. Would the world in general and the United States in particular be better off without the just war doctrine and tradition? The practitioners (and benefactors) of this sophistry seem troubled by a theory that sets out to militate against the evil of war. That it can be used to enhance the imperial ambitions of specific states is something—to paraphrase Stanley Hoffmann—that is smuggled in. Seeing no flaws in the present system, James Turner Johnson would build on it without checking on how the foundation is holding: "The real challenge held out by the contemporary rediscovery of just war thought as a source of moral wisdom is to develop much more discriminating, more proportional means of warfare. In the present contest this implies more reliance upon conventional forces (even with the moral difficulties posed by some conventional arms), upon civil defense, and upon physical separation of military from centers of civilian population. All these are politically (in the ideological sense of that word) unpopular. The challenge then becomes one of how to make the morally preferable also politically possible."[15] Walzer, to be sure, is perfectly aware of this problem: "Just wars are limited

---

15. Johnson, *Just War Tradition and the Restraint of War,* 366.

wars; there are moral reasons for the statesman and soldiers who fight them to be prudent and realistic. Overreaching is common in war, however, and has many causes. I do not want to deny that a certain characteristic distortion of the argument for justice is one among them."[16]

Finally, in this critique of the just war, one needs to abandon the just war framework altogether. So far, I have stayed within all the parameters and made objections to the just war theory on its own terms. The real problem, however, is with the idea itself in the modern age. No nation nowadays will enter a war simply because it is just. Here is where the realist position comes to the rescue. "Just war" may be a necessary cry to mobilize American public opinion, but it is not alone sufficient to cause a wise leader to plunge the nation into bloody conflict. The realist tripod—clear national interest, augmentation of power, and a moral choice after analyzing the issue—will be a surer guide to justifying a decision to go to war today. A just war pronouncement is now simply a symbol used by both sides of any war, even the 1991 Gulf War. Since Napoleon, wars have been waged on a national scale—every citizen is a cog in the gross national war effort. World War II was perhaps the ultimate expression of that fact. If everyone's war is just, then those who believe they must go to war, out of necessity, fear, or honor, should turn to realism for policy and to just war theory for propaganda and self-delusion.

An even more basic criticism of the concentration on the just war as a way to improve international morality comes from Luigi Bonanate of Italy in his book *Ethics and International Politics.* He picks up on Carl von Clausewitz's dictum that war is a continuation of politics by other means and the need, or at least the opportunity, to judge the right or wrong of war at an earlier stage. Clausewitz wrote: "War never breaks out wholly unexpectedly, nor can it spread instantaneously. Each side can therefore gauge the other to a large extent by what he is and does, instead of judging him by what he, strictly speaking, ought to be or do." Bonanate then asks, "If war is not an isolated, self-contained act, but the continuation of policy by other means, shouldn't we apply our criteria to politics and not to war? Only if it is intertwined with politics can war be explained."[17]

Having located just war theory in religion (or spirituality) in the first instance, I find it appropriate to turn to that quarter. What should we ask religion to do? Should we urge an ecumenical conference to ensure that some new body

16. Walzer, *Just and Unjust Wars,* 122.

17. Luigi Bonanate, *Ethics and International Politics,* trans. John Irving (Columbia: University of South Carolina Press, 1995).

guarantees the implementation of each step of *jus ad bellum* so that *jus in bello* is rarely needed? Or should we propose that religious and secular forces together, brandishing their twin swords, carve up new territory but use extant organizations at regional and international levels to head off war altogether, or, at a minimum, to certify the justice of every conflict? Or do we worry with Reinhold Niebuhr that the quality of morality worsens as we progress from the individual to each higher level of collective vision?

Pope John Paul II is of some help here, although not on the issue of new collective restraints. "Man is always the same. The systems he creates are always imperfect, and the more imperfect they are, the more he is sure of himself."[18] In reference to just war theory, the remembrance of La Belle Epoque, a phrase of a hundred years ago, is haunting. Progress was the new religion and war was impossible. There were three reasons for this claim: economic ties, the solidarity of the working class (cutting across national boundaries), and the technology of modern warfare. Andrew Carnegie, the steel magnate and philanthropist, hoped to add a fourth restraint, the Christian religion common to the Teutonic powers—Germany, Great Britain, and the United States. Nonetheless, this brief epoch was followed by World War I, World War II, and about fifty years of the Cold War. The question yet to be answered is, Are we leaving the Cold War for peace or for another round of war? Just war theory has no predictive powers, and justice is always in short supply and often an easy victim. Nuclear weapons still abound, and a major "just war" could jeopardize all the apparent gains of the end of the Cold War.

Another quarrel with the just war concept is that it moralizes great human tragedy, turning every war into someone's crusade. For Woodrow Wilson, World War I was a crusade to end war and to make the world safe for democracy; Franklin D. Roosevelt's rhetoric in World War II was no less moralistic (he believed, for example, that the war would "cleanse the world of ancient evils, ancient ills"); and, as we have seen in more detail, even Vietnam, an essentially unheroic battle with a Third World country, assumed the cast of moral necessity. There may well be situations in which a crusading spirit is necessary, but the just war idea makes it all too easy to legitimize excess and to blur the vision of the leaders who are entrusted with the question of war and peace. Morgenthau established the first of his four fundamental principles of diplomacy—that it "must be divested of the Crusading Spirit"—so that the conduct of war, when necessary, concentrates on purpose, interest, and strategy.

---

18. Pope John Paul II, *Crossing the Threshold of Hope* (New York: Knopf, 1994), 6.

It may be worth pondering a fuller statement on war and just war by August-ine, who brings a quiet skepticism to the subject:

> If I were to try to describe, with an eloquence worthy of the subject, the many and multifarious distresses, the dour and dire necessities, I could not possibly be ade-quate to the theme, and there would be no end to the protracted discussion. But the wise man, they say, will wage just wars. Surely, if he remembers that he is a human being, he will rather lament the fact that he is faced with the necessity of wars , for if they were not just, he would not have to engage in them, and conse-quently there would be no wars for a wise man. For it is the injustice of the oppos-ing side that lays on the wise man the duty of waging wars; and this injustice is as-suredly to be deplored by a human being, since it is the injustice of human beings, even though no necessity for war should arise from it. And so everyone who re-flects with sorrow on such previous ills, in all their horror and cruelty, must ac-knowledge the misery of them. And yet a man who experiences such evils, or even thinks about them, without heartfelt grief, is assuredly in a far more pitiable condi-tion, if he thinks himself happy simply because he has lost all human feeling.[19]

On balance, how should one judge the moral weight of the just war criteria in moderating conflict, say, in the next century? In reviewing the ideal conditions and interpretations of the just war doctrine, it is difficult to quarrel with the in-tention. That the formula is misused does not necessarily invalidate the doc-trine. Yet in a world of sovereign states, a formula whose righteousness is in the eye of the beholder is surely fatally flawed. Just war theory provides the oppor-tunity and pseudo-justification for the evil Augustine describes so eloquently. The unctuousness and hypocrisy associated with the soldier priests and politi-cians cast a dark shadow over the integrity of language and morality. Adding new words to the old formula will not do. We simply have to face the inevitabil-ity of war and the fact that war is hostile to measured conceptions of justice. We have a choice between the Weberian ethic of conviction (the crusade) and the thought of consequences, a utilitarian measure whose morality stops at half-plus-one. The just war criteria may not contribute to that final decision.

To recall the James Johnson system, the logic of war would ideally return to a single champion representing each warring party. But these David and Goliath determinations have little to do with justice, if the idea of war is all about some-how seeing that a universal justice is served. Constraints on war through the cultivation of virtue—wisdom, justice, courage, and moderation—may some-day lead to statecraft that weighs the options and explains every peaceful alter-native. (McNamara regrets that he did not.)

---

19. Augustine, *City of God* (London: Penguin, 1984), Book XIX, Chap. 7, pp. 861–62.

In this case, the "last resort" occurs with less frequency. But the end of war as a human enterprise exceeds mortal grasp. One could perhaps imagine a peaceful society of which an absolute self-endorsed code for handling war was an integral part so that the conditions of society as a whole set the standards for its performance in peace and war. Is such a self-regulating society possible? For the time being, perhaps all we can do is to remember to place quotation marks around "just war." As Erasmus put it, "The good Christian Prince should hold under suspicion every war, no matter how just."

The Machiavellian argument for actions of the state under the banner of *necessito* seems a stronger justification for a state going to war than the flabby, malleable language of the just war. In brief, *necessito* requires a stiff definition of "national interest" if the state wishes to assure itself of the support of its citizens. Crusades are less likely. The decision or policy takes on an air of realism. This will be considered further in the concluding chapter. Before then, we will explore the damage that the idea of just war contributes to the prospects for such institutions as the UN to find normative standards around which states can coalesce in a genuine sense of world community.

7 The UN and the Realists: The Misapplication of International Organization

During the savage struggle of World War II, the primacy of the wisdom of political realism seemed to have been learned. Interest, power, and morality interlocked in the councils of the principal Allied powers. The Soviet Union was a valuable ally in the war against the Axis. It was the aim of the United States, through both FDR and Harry Hopkins, to see to it that this alliance continued into the postwar world; the United States was prepared to take considerable risks to convert the Soviet Union into a cooperative power against the presumed greater good of a brave new world. The U.S. secretary of state, Cordell Hull, was convinced that most U.S. defense needs could be met through the new Security Council of the UN composed of the five remaining great powers, the United States, the USSR, China, France, and Britain. In the euphoria of victory, the idea that common interests would prevail was tentatively accepted. The intransigence of the Soviet Union, especially over Eastern Europe, where its military power prevailed, demonstrated to all who would look and listen that everyone was not marching to the same drummer. To abandon "national interest" in favor of some vague collaboration did not appeal for a moment to the realists. Wartime cooperation to defeat the Axis was clearly important; but that war having concluded, what reason was there to anticipate that close (but flawed) cooperation would prevail in the future? Disagreements over Berlin and Eastern Europe set the scene for Winston Churchill's "Iron Curtain" speech, and the attack by North Korea on South Korea on 25 June 1950 marked the limited cooperation that could be expected from the UN in the security field. Not until the end of the Cold War were broader horizons reopened, although even then with major qualifications. Realism rose once again to save the day for the democracies in that it instigated the common concern in the West for freedom and security and produced such institutions as NATO (the shield of the West), rearmed America, and virtually drove out idealism and various neo- relatives from the top councils of Western politicians.

Nonetheless, the UN has existed for over fifty years. The fiftieth anniversary was celebrated in 1995, and from that perspective, it is valuable to review the project to make some judgments as well as to project its future possibilities. The organization was formed in San Francisco in the waning days of the war and then inaugurated and opened for business on 24 October 1945 in New York City. Fifty years later, in a celebratory mode, some 140 chiefs of state or government met at the UN headquarters in New York. The briefness of the speeches characterized not only the traffic congestion but the paucity of important security accomplishments. The litany was one of complaint and not hosannas. It is worth examining these speeches to see what are the various interests of the members and whether a body such as the UN is the proper vehicle to achieve them. Among the philosophers we have so far considered, only Kant would appear to have been willing to trust in an international organization to deal with the real conflicts that roil international relations.

The celebration first in San Francisco and then in New York might well be characterized as the "words and deeds" of the United Nations. The October meeting pointed up the need for reforms but also, in a very concrete way, highlighted not only the roots of discontent from the viewpoint of the great powers but also the lamentations of the weak who look to particular possibilities in the UN Charter that they feel are not being realized. The Tower of Babel aspects of the behemoth on the edge of the East River have never been more forcefully articulated, even as the speakers by and large tried to dwell on the achievements and possibilities rather than the disappointments and failures. We will concentrate on the questions that lie on the surface, or in some cases those that are obscured, as we analyze only five categories: great power rivalries in the Security Council; issues of power sharing from the perspective of small states; the questions of social justice and income distribution; problems of dependency and colonialism from the perspective of the twenty-first century; and disarmament and arms control.

When the UN began, there were 51 members of the General Assembly. That number has now reached 185 and is growing as new states are created mainly by succession through the breakup of multicultural states, under some version of the Wilsonian slogan of "self-determination." There seems to be no end in sight of this process, which plays to the ego and individuality of subgroups of humanity to the detriment of the larger community. This is the counterpart of the traditional struggle of the individual against the society in general that manifests itself, for example, in some of the burning social problems of America, all revolving around the proper role for government in both domestic and international society.

Foreseeing the proliferation of nation-states, the founders placed at the heart of the UN the Security Council. This permanent group was composed of five nations, the winning coalition that defeated the Axis in Europe, Germany and Italy, as well as their ally in Asia, Japan. The original Security Council reflected the principal powers of the day, although in the case of China, it was not long until the results of the Chinese civil war made moot the role of the Republic of China as it moved from the mainland to Taiwan in 1949. It is no longer an open question that the current lineup of permanent Security Council members (the original group) does not represent the current balance of power. The intrinsic strength of both Germany and Japan, and perhaps others such as India and Brazil, in a new alignment of the nation-states, may have to be recognized. (There are now ten nonpermanent, rotating members of the Security Council. They have a vote but no veto.)

Is this a permanent condition or is there some way out? The answer is not clear, but it is a delicate issue. There is a mechanism in the UN Charter to bring about institutional reform through Article 100, which provides for "a General Conference of the Members of the United Nations for the purpose of reviewing the present charter."[1] While those reform procedures are available, so far, none of the members of the Security Council has taken the initiative, which would be the only way to attempt such a change. (More consideration of this problem is reserved for later in this chapter.)

Reforming the UN Charter has roughly the same political hazards as exist on the domestic level in the United States of amending the Constitution. The "special interests" can be expected to bring in their favorite proposals—which our discussion will demonstrate to be almost unending—and the outcome might well be worse than the present system. The problem of course is not what many claim it to be, a simple need for some administrative tinkering that will set wrong things right. The complaints actually go to the heart of the inherent difficulties of dealing with sovereign states. Sovereignty by definition means that there is no outside power that can enforce its will on the sovereign. Power is the commodity, and it can be trumped only by superior power. This means that the major powers are basically exempt from the system and that the only subjects to Security Council mandates are the weak, a version of the old Melian dialogue all

---

1. Also see Wendell Gordon, *The United Nations at the Crossroads of Reform* (London: M. E. Sharpe, 1994), Chap. 15.

over again. We shall see how this works and learn the current attitudes of the actors by examining more closely the five categories of problems listed above.

As the host to the celebration, President Bill Clinton was allowed nine instead of five minutes to pay tribute to the UN and to emphasize his priorities. "The United Nations is the product of faith and knowledge—faith that different people can work together for tolerance, decency, and peace. Knowledge that this faith will be forever tested by the forces of intolerance, depravity, and aggression." This statement set a defensive tone for the onslaught of arguments to come. Clinton continued: "Now we must summon that faith and act on the knowledge to meet the challenges of a new era. In the United States, some people ask, 'Why should we bother with the U.N.? America is strong. We can go it alone.'

"Well, we will act if we have to alone, but my fellow Americans should not forget that our values and our interests are also served by working with the U.N.

"The U.N. helps the peace makers, the care providers, the defenders of freedom and human rights, the architects of economic prosperity, and the protection of our planet to spread the risk, share the burden, and increase the impact of our common efforts." Clinton assured the audience that the massive U.S. financial arrears in dues (over $1 billion) were being negotiated with Congress, although at the same time, the UN needed to cut back expenses and become more efficient. And finally, "Throughout this hemisphere, every nation except one has chosen democracy, and the goal of an integrated peaceful and democratic Europe is now within our reach for the first time. In the Balkans, the international community's determination and NATO's resolve have made prospects for peace brighter than they have been for four long years."[2]

The UN in its complexities and possibilities is reminiscent of the Indian tale of the blind man describing an elephant, his description varying depending on which part of the beast's apparatus he seized. Russian president Boris Yeltsin revealed a perspective different from Clinton's. "There is a dangerous tendency," Yeltsin said, "to play down the role of the United Nations, to circumvent its charter and the collective will of the Security Council."[3]

"Today the world, more than ever before, needs not only equality and tolerance, but respect for the identity of each state and an understanding of the peculiar features of its history. Each of them can and is willing to make its contribution to the development of the world community, and to find a worthy place therein. We should not allow the revival of the atmosphere of animosity and

2. *New York Times*, 23 October 1995.
3. Ibid.

prejudice against countries and peoples." Yeltsin then posed a rhetorical question: does the UN have the ability to achieve these goals? "In the opinion of Russia, it does. The United Nations can and should become the main instrument for building new international relations. It has all the necessary power to do so. To carry out this mission, it should be provided with appropriate means, including financial resources. Russia meets and continues to meet its obligations to the United Nations." He continued: "Certainly the United Nations has not been able to achieve success in all areas, but the roots of its failures first and foremost lie in ourselves and the behavior of states and organizations. Russia is concerned at the situation whereby, as has recently been the case in Bosnia, the Security Council was relegated to the sidelines of events, it represents an obvious and clear-cut violation of the foundations of the world organization laid down by its founders." Here his complaint was pointed. "It is inadmissible for a regional organization to take decisions on the mass use of force bypassing the Security Council. Russia has worked hard to bring closer peace in Bosnia and Herzegovina. We are ready to support the operation on the implementation of a peace agreement with the participation of multinational forces, but only after a clear-cut mandate of the United Nations Security Council." Military force, Yeltsin said, "should never be used in those cases where diplomacy has proved unable to succeed. The effects of that would be tragic."[4] He went on to say:

> The main concern of Russia is to achieve stability in Europe and Asia. We are in favor of establishing a security system based on compromises rather than pressure. European security is indivisible. There is no alternative to that.
>
> This is precisely the reason why Russia supports the idea of the earliest establishment of a new system of all European security where all European states would be represented. And this is precisely the reason why we are against NATO's eastern expansion. It will put a barrier on the way to establishing a unified Europe.
>
> The question is an extremely acute one. Either such a system would be established for all Europe or as in the past, only for a select few. The strengthening of one bloc today means new confrontation beginning tomorrow.[5]

So far, however, the Russians through 1997 have acquiesced in the first step in the expansion of NATO, adding as it did Poland, Hungary, and the Czech Republic.

In the context of the whole meeting, the statements of Clinton and Yeltsin touch on the five issues I raised as causing tension in the world body. There is

---

4. Ibid.
5. Ibid.

built in a thorny problem of power and prestige by having two bodies: the power level, the Security Council; and the prestige level (for the minor players), the General Assembly. In the latter each state has one vote, but all the important matters, especially dealing with peace and security, rest with the Security Council, as spelled out in the UN Charter. At first this arrangement was considered progressive, a change from the League of Nations Charter, which required unanimity on security decisions, so everyone had a veto. Here there were only five with a claim to having earned a superior role. There was an effort to placate the disgruntled by adding first six and then ten nonpermanent members of the Security Council without veto rights. But nonetheless, on matters of war and peace, only the five permanent members needed to agree.

This formula of the UN, however, proved no less difficult in practice than that of the League. FDR and Cordell Hull, his secretary of state, had gone to great lengths at Yalta in February 1945 to persuade Stalin to cooperate in a new postwar world, thereby ushering in a period of unprecedented collaboration. This was to begin in Europe. Decisions to give the USSR a favored position in Eastern Europe to satisfy Stalin's demands proved to be shortsighted, and almost fifty years were required to right those wrongs. This is illustrative, however, of the high hopes in some quarters that a truly new system of international relations was not only possible but desirable, idealism once again unwilling to look the world straight in the face. This miscalculation, as it turned out, provided the impetus for a return of realism with its emphasis on national interest, power, and morality. The old paradigm of power politics, with its virtues and vices discussed in the Introduction, once again stood the West in good stead.

This old philosophy was altogether relevant for the five powers in their quest for the principle of unanimity in their deliberations in the Security Council. Some way had to be found in traditional politics, in the spirit of negotiation and compromise, to deal with the veto principle. The veto was unpopular on two levels. The first came from the second- and third-tier members of the General Assembly, who felt that both their prestige and power were placed at a certain risk when the discriminatory authority of the Security Council was so blatant, and the second from the Security Council members themselves, who saw the unanimity requirement as both a blessing and a curse.

The blessing came from a growing appreciation of the reality of realism. Important issues of war and peace had to meet in some degree the interests of all five members. These calculations by the national leaders in a spirit of give-and-take, a willingness to yield or compromise on matters that were not vital to their national survival, provided the parameters for agreement. In this sense, the unanimity idea raised the possibility of being a positive political principle.

Because of the hardening ideology of the Cold War, however, by the time the members moved into their new home on New York City's East River in December 1950, ideas of compromise and negotiation were no longer fashionable. The Korea "police action" of June 1950 was sponsored by the UN only because the USSR was (unwisely as it turned out) boycotting the Security Council and so could cast no vote on sanctions against North Korea. This demonstrated the real division between East and West that characterized the UN during the long years of the Cold War. Progress was still possible in the functional agencies, such as the World Health Organization, UNESCO, UNICEF, the World Bank, and the International Monetary Fund. But for the Security Council to act as a concert of powers, in the nineteenth-century tradition, proved elusive. By 1995, on the occasion of the fiftieth anniversary, the United States and Russia contented themselves, as we have seen in Clinton's and Yeltsin's speeches, with glancing blows in their less intense rivalry at that historic moment.

At the anniversary, complaints about the inherently unfair status of the Security Council persisted. Criticism along those lines came from Fidel Castro, the Cuban leader, who saw in this arrangement a "new colonialism." Although Cuba remains one of the chief Third World arms buyers (about $9 billion annually), he favored the elimination of weapons of mass destruction and was against the "use of force, arrogance, and pressure in international relations." Further, it was his view that "the obsolete veto privilege and the ill use of the Security Council by the powerful are exalting a new colonialism within the very United Nations. Latin America and Africa do not have one single permanent member on the Security Council. In Asia, India has a population of about almost two billion [*sic*], but it does not enjoy that responsibility."[6]

Rallying against an imposed universalism, Castro concluded: "We lay claim to a world without hegemonism, without nuclear weapons, without interventionism, without racism, without national or religious hatred, without outrageous acts against the sovereignty of any country—a world of respect for the independence and self-determination of people, a world without universal models that totally disregard the traditions and culture of all the components of mankind."[7]

In regard to the economic distributionist features of the UN, in the economic and social fields, the president of Sri Lanka, Chandrika Bandaranaike Kurmaratunga, raised the important question of whether peacekeeping expenditures would replace traditional economic development funds. (The rush by certain

6. Ibid.
7. Ibid.

UN bureaucrats in 1993 to change the Somali mission from humanitarian aid to "nation building" revealed a new aid strategy that was soon rejected.)

> Under the principle of the Declaration on the Right to Development, adopted in 1986, measures are applied positively with the full commitment of the developed and developing countries; otherwise, the developmental process will not be sufficiently advanced.
>
> Such an effective improvement requires in our view, that, firstly, development priorities should not be sacrificed to the pursuit of political military operations which must be set at realistic even modest levels.
>
> Secondly, decision-making by the United Nations in all areas must be based on full engagement of all members. The Security Council, in particular, must become more representative and more responsive to the general membership of the United Nations.
>
> Thirdly, commitments made for multilateral actions in all fields must be honored and diligently pursued. In short, the revitalizing forces must have the capacity of the United Nations rather than merely effect economies and scale down its scope.[8]

Among the litany of complaints and point-scoring among the chief competitors were the upbeat remarks of President Kim Young Sam of South Korea. "The Republic of Korea was established in accordance with a U.N. resolution in 1948. At that time it was one of the poorest countries in the world. Today, it is the 11th largest economy in the world and a truly democratic nation. Our success has been a great manifestation of the ideals of the United Nations."[9] President Kim recounted the participation of South Korea in peacekeeping operations and developmental and environmental projects. Also, Korea proposed to increase its financial contribution to the UN. He concluded by calling on the UN to support the peaceful reunification of the Korean peninsula. With but five minutes to speak, he had no time to mention the downside of UN involvement in Korea. In 1948, elections were held only in the south under UN supervision; above the thirty-eighth parallel, the Soviets, then occupying the north, and the North Koreans refused to participate in UN-sponsored elections, thereby perpetuating the division between south and north and preparing the way for the devastating Korean War.

The UN section having to do with disarmament and arms control has from the beginning faced the most difficult tasks. There are bizarre reasons for this, but the popular demand for progress in this area goes on unabated. In the

8. Ibid.
9. Ibid.

United States, for example, at the grass-roots level, the control of both nuclear and conventional weapons is high on citizen groups' list of concerns. Even the old arguments in the 1930s of Senator Burton K. Wheeler are raised anew and the outcries against the merchants of death have lost none of their vigor. Why arms control poses such difficulty, especially if one wishes to enlist the services of the UN, is revealed in an interview with Oscar Arias, former president of Costa Rica, who was awarded the Nobel Peace Prize for his role in ending the civil wars in both Nicaragua and El Salvador in 1987. Now in his mid-fifties, Arias continues to work for peace through the Costa Rica–based Arias Foundation for Peace and Human Progress.[10] He had tried to encourage two points: the elimination of armies when they are manifestly not needed (a variation of Kant's drive to eliminate standing armies), and the discouragement of First World powers from selling weapons to Third World countries. The combination of these two efforts should reduce the expenditure of funds that Arias believes should be used for better purposes. There has not, however, been any movement in this direction.

In response to why he is now concentrating on the arms trade, Arias replied: "In recent years, world military spending has decreased. It's gone from $1 trillion annually in 1967 to $750 billion in 1994. But what everyone was predicting, a 'peace dividend,' from that savings hasn't appeared. Lots of developed countries have cut their military budgets, but the savings have been used to cut government spending to eliminate budget deficits, anything but to help the world's poorest countries—Asia, Africa and Latin America—which during the cold war received attention and help from the superpowers." He elaborated on this point. "The developed countries still keep selling enormous quantities of arms to Third World countries which are spending $229 billion annually on their military budgets. This is more than four times what they get in foreign aid. Or to put it another way, 12 percent of the developing nations' annual military spending would pay the cost of health care for all of the world's people. It would pay for immunization for all children, the elimination of severe malnutrition and the provision of safe drinking water for all."[11]

At that time Arias was proposing a global demilitarization fund, based on a proposal for a 3 percent annual reduction of military budgets everywhere and then taking one-tenth of that to set up the fund. The hurdles along this path are very high, and help from the UN as an organization is dim. Why is this so? "Last year, for [arms sales] the world total was $35.6 billion; of that the Third

---

10. This interview was published on 29 October 1995 in the *San Francisco Chronicle*.
11. Ibid.

World bought 70 percent, $25.4 billion dollars. In the 1990s, more than 90 percent of the arms sold to developing countries were supplied by the five permanent members of the UN Security Council, plus Germany. And in the last four years, the United States has been the main supplier to the Third World, averaging about $15 billion of sales to those nations." Arias concluded his case as follows: "You know that some day those arms can fire against American soldiers. The boomerang effect of the arms trade will be more poverty, more inequality, more terrorism, more illegal immigration."[12]

From the perspective of realism, one looks in vain for how such a body can be expected to cope with the passions and aspirations of such a disparate group. On reading the sampling of statements of various world leaders on the occasion of the UN's fiftieth birthday, one can easily see the difference in interests, which cannot be papered over. The struggles for power and dominance in the Security Council and in the General Assembly are quite different aspirations, preferring, for example, aid to peacekeeping and the Kantian hopes for the recognition of universal against country-specific ethnicity and the nationalism of a Fidel Castro. This is also highlighted in the case of human rights, the subject of the Universal Declaration of Human Rights in 1948, struggling against the particularists.

Hanging above all of this is the statement of Pope John Paul II that should be emblazoned on a banner hung across the vast auditorium of the General Assembly: "Man is always the same. The systems he creates are always imperfect, and the more imperfect they are, the more he is sure of himself."

From the realist perspective, the UN mechanism provides the strong with an additional means to overcome the weak. The same mechanism, however, under certain circumstances can be used as a weapon of the weak, as happened in the end in the case of Somalia. Utilitarianism, the enemy of Kant and his principles, tries to develop consequentially laden schemes to provide its supporters with an argument of logic and leverage. And this theme too ran through the brief encounters with a variety of leaders at the UN birthday party. Because a majority of the 185 nations behave in a manner Castro professes to prefer, each to his own self being true, the idea of forming real consensus based on core values has seldom been realized. The Universal Declaration of Human Rights proclaimed in 1948 when the number of countries involved shared some basic notions of civilization, as John Stuart Mill would recommend, is under attack. In late July 1997, Malaysian prime minister Mahathir, at a meeting of the Association of

12. Ibid.

Southeast Asian Nations, suggested repealing the Universal Declaration of Human Rights. He thought it did not reflect "Asian values."[13]

It is precisely because the Universal Declaration of Human Rights proposes to humanize and provide a helping hand to all humanity that it is unique. Working at times against the interests of both the powerful and the bigoted, it receives only modest support. Japan, for all its desire to play a larger international role commensurate with its financial power, has moved over the past two years from supporting the Declaration of Human Rights to a view closer to that of China, Malaysia, North Korea, and Castro, that human rights are everyone's internal affair. Human rights is a truly revolutionary way to conduct politics on the planet and is a genuine threat to statism. This has positive and negative aspects, which will be considered at greater length in Chapter 9.

The current disagreement over human rights (apparently settled in 1948) demonstrates the possibilities as well as the hazards for progress in finding common ground. One of the values, perhaps more potential than yet realized, is that through the over fifty years of experience there is an area of agreement that may provide the basis for an "international community." This has reinforced the precedent of previous centuries of international protocols; many were violated under the "scrap of paper" doctrine of the European powers, but despite the abuses, there seems to be a "core code" that can be constructed from the experience and interactions of states in the daily flow of international life.

Dorothy V. Jones, in her book *Code of Peace: Ethics and Security in the World of the Warlord States*, lists eight basic and two auxiliary principles that the concert of states have agreed on through various international negotiations over time. The eight principles are sovereign equality of states; territorial integrity and political independence of states; equal rights and self-determination of people; nonintervention in the internal affairs of states; peaceful settlement of disputes between states; abstention from the threat or use of force; fulfillment in good faith of international obligations; and respect for human rights and fundamental freedoms. The auxiliary principles, which still do not have universal agreement, are creation of an equitable international economic order and protection of the environment.[14]

From the realist perspective, this level of agreement may seem specious, although here one can refer to Martin Wight's idea of what views various people

---

13. *New York Times*, 3 August 1997.

14. Dorothy V. Jones, *Code of Peace: Ethics and Security in the World of the Warlord States* (Chicago: University of Chicago Press, 1991), 163–64.

carry with them. To UN critics, the progress and reforms that are proposed, from both inside and outside the system, may seem almost frivolous, often because of the need for finding the shaky common ground. The limitations on what the UN can do as a body created by sovereign states and beholden to them are self-evident, despite the occasional lament by former secretary general Boutros Boutros Ghali that somehow the UN as an institution should have more power.[15] Article 2, paragraph 7, of the charter states, "Nothing contained in the present charter shall authorize the United Nations to intervene in matters which are essentially within the domestic jurisdiction of any state or shall require the Members to submit such matters to settlement under the present charter, but this principle shall not prejudice the application of enforcement measures under Chapter VII" (the chapter titled "Action with Respect to Threats to the Peace, Breaches of the Peace, and Acts of Aggression"). Article 2, paragraph 7, is, however, absolutely essential to the success of the organization because few nations would sign on otherwise. One could imagine the hue and cry from the U.S. Congress and the executive branch as well without such a disclaimer.

For those intent on replacing the nation-state system with a cosmopolitan alternative, Article 2, paragraph 7, should be removed altogether. Sovereign authority would pass to the UN, and it would, in that case, become a true world government. It could delegate certain powers to individual states and would also be in a position to take them back. Such a system would be a rough replica of the U.S. federal and state system. So in the range between the solution and the present reality, reformers remain busy with matters around the edges. Those keen on world government would in effect seek a "constitutional change," a new charter, while others would seek political deals and procedural innovations. The 1997 addition of a deputy secretary general is an example of the latter.

The need or demand for change was not overlooked by the UN founders. Article 100 was the chosen instrument, providing for a "General Conference of the Members of the United Nations for the purpose of reviewing the present charter." If no such conference is held after ten years, then the General Assembly is to place this matter on its agenda. Some UN observers took heart when President George Bush, in the euphoria of the Gulf War, spoke of the need for creating a "New World Order." So far, that impulse has not been the signal for convoking such a conference, and after fifty years, no such review has been held for the purpose of making changes in the charter. This does not mean, however,

15. See *San Francisco Chronicle*, 22 October 1996.

that a great number of changes have not been suggested by a variety of interests.[16]

A thoughtful argument was put forward by former secretary of state Cyrus R. Vance, who is not unaware of the complexity of the UN dilemma: "I believe that a Charter Review Conference could serve a useful purpose for at least two major reasons. First, as good as it is—and the Charter is indeed a far-sighted document—fifty years have passed since the adoption. A half-century is a long time in the life of any organization, and I think the Charter merits another close examination. . . . What kind of a United Nations do we want? A Charter Review Conference would and should take time—perhaps four or five years—and while it is deliberating, the necessary reforms and restructuring of the organization could proceed."[17]

Some call for changes in the composition of the Security Council permanent members by adding some of the World War II losers such as Japan and Germany. Others would add India and Brazil on the basis of size, population, and importance. One can see how this might augment the power and prestige of these countries, especially Japan, which seems eager to find new ways to increase its power under the guise of absorbing unwanted responsibility. Enlarging the number of permanent members might create a more effective international balance, but it is difficult to make a case that this aspect of the charter alone is the main obstacle to a more effective UN.

A study by the United Nations Association makes a case for reform, but a cautious one indeed: "While institutional changes are clearly needed, a balance has to be struck between what is available now and what may be desirable ultimately."[18] Some of these steps (from the American viewpoint) should be in the image of the American corporation, downsizing staff and chopping the overhead. Here the smaller states, as noted above in the case of Sri Lanka, are very much opposed to reduction of the UN staff and budget and prefer higher appropriations for their favorite projects. UNESCO in the 1980s was a particularly blatant example of waste, nepotism, and general corruption, compelling the United States and other nations to withdraw from it. Only the vigorous efforts

---

16. For a compilation, see Gordon, *United Nations at the Crossroads of Reform.*

17. National Committee on American Foreign Policy, "What Kind of United Nations Do We Want?" (New York City, 21 November 1995), 18.

18. Peter J. Fromuth, "Executive Summary," *A Successor Vision: The United Nations of Tomorrow*, ed. Fromuth (New York: United Nations Association of the United States of America, University Press of America, 1988), xviii.

of the Spaniard Fedrico Major, its present director, saved the day and show promise of carrying out its humanitarian and cultural mandate.

Also in the 1980s as the Cold War (unnoticed) was reaching a crescendo, the Palme commission (chaired by Olaf Palme, twice prime minister of Sweden) tried to come to grips with both disarmament and peacekeeping. Two of his recommendations were that (1) "a doctrine of common security must replace the present expedient of deterrence through armaments. International peace must rest on the commitment to joint survival rather than a threat of mutual destruction, and (2) the Commission strongly supports the goal of general and complete disarmament."[19]

The most ambitious paper reform occurred in 1992, when the Security Council, chaired by John Major, the former British prime minister, requested that the then-new UN secretary general Boutros Boutros Ghali make recommendations (short of calling for a charter-rewriting conference). Boutros Ghali did not touch Article 2, paragraph 7, and said early in his report: "The foundation stone of this work is and must remain the State. Respect for its fundamental sovereignty and integrity [is] crucial to any common international progress. The time of absolute and exclusive sovereignty, however, has passed; its theory was never matched by reality." However true that may be, the recommendations there and in the charter that troops be available to the UN command have never been approved. Boutros Ghali was also responsible for a September 1993 "Report on the Work of the General Assembly." No new ground was broken here, and in my view, no matter how many UN-sponsored studies are issued, no significant change will happen. Only some contingency that provokes the Security Council to action will be sufficient.

The root problem—if problem it is—comes from those who wish to turn the UN into something it is not, namely a world government. For these people the roadblock is state sovereignty. This particular conundrum was debated in 1949 between Robert Hutchins, former president of the University of Chicago, and Reinhold Niebuhr, the Lutheran theologian. Hutchins was characteristically impatient with anyone who did not agree with him. In Hutchins's view, the imperative of the atomic bomb, still an American monopoly but a monopoly that could not be sustained, required a world government; such a scheme was inevitable, so the only thing to do was to get on with it. Niebuhr, on the other hand, argued that the conditions for a world government were incomplete. There would first have to be established a real world community, analogous to the na-

19. *The Palme Commission Report* (New York: Simon and Schuster, 1982).

tion-state, that combined common values and purposes, laws, mores, and habits. Hutchins replied that it was this kind of thinking that stood in the way of world government. Niebuhr thought that under current conditions, attention to the familiar balance of power was the best recourse. Hutchins quoted Confucius: "Men cannot work together unless they have common principles," which would seem to support Niebuhr's argument. But Hutchins followed by saying that Niebuhr exaggerated the state of perfection which the world community had to achieve before world government could be considered.[20] The atomic bomb for Hutchins was the *deus ex machina* and hence his one note moralizing on the danger of the bomb. The danger to the world from nuclear weapons still exists, but the attitude of the nuclear powers is less threatening. Obviously, to date, the world powers, nuclear and non-nuclear, are willing to exist in a twilight peace while efforts to strengthen cooperative control over nuclear matters continue.

In other substantive matters, the international system as embodied in the UN can do only what the Security Council in its unanimity wishes it to do. That is the reality. So it is not surprising that the UN apparatus does not have in its own right an independent military or a high-tech communications facility. In November 1995 there were seventy separate proposals to revise the Security Council. Most focused on adding more nonpermanent members as well as abolishing the veto. No action has yet been taken. Wendell Gordon is among those who take a dim view of the current situation: "The United Nations should have the power to impose peace. It is to be hoped that it would also have the judgment to take action in a manner conducive to the existence of civilized society as a consequence of such action. Initially, however, the United Nations (not the United States, Russia or China) must possess a dominating military power. After the nations 'get the idea,' the UN will surely need to maintain less military forces on a permanent basis."[21] The implication here is that the behemoth on the East River has prevailed and is now the master of the universe. From the realist perspective, no such scenario is likely. Progress toward world community is more likely to proceed according to Max Weber's approach to politics: "Politics is a strong and slow boring of hard boards."

Having survived the intellectual assaults of a variety of historicisms, especially in the nineteenth century, historic realism so far has not yielded to the lure of international organization as the way out of international political di-

---

20. Saul H. Mendlovitz, *Legal and Political Problems of World Order* (New York: Fund for Education Concerning World Peace through World Law, 1962), 66–67.

21. Gordon, *United Nations at the Crossroads of Reform*, 224.

lemmas. It has in fact made possible what progress there has been in the functional side of UN activities. Yet still new challenges arise, particularly novel ways of articulating power through people's movements such as environmental groups and human rights activists. These new events are significant because they demonstrate the various forms that politics assumes to advance specific interests. Realism takes these all seriously into account.

8   The Perplexing Problem of Intervention

The question of whether armed conflict or war is "just" seems to be more a matter of self-cognition and influence molding than of advancing a particular set of national interests. The appeal to "justice" satisfies only limited ends; a real sovereign war, however, not only requires a high quality of public relations but in the end must be based on self-interest, an accrual of more power, and a morally satisfactory choice available to the statesman. Assuming that the opponent in a war is of substantial strength (or why is war necessary?), there is a high level of risk and sacrifice. War cannot be undertaken lightly. High Kantian imperatives are not likely to carry the day if the war itself begins to smell of failure, as in Korea in 1950 or Vietnam in the mid-1960s, and the costs begin to exceed the prospects of comparable gain. True, neither Korea nor Vietnam was technically a war, but the high public profile and perception placed them in that category. The size and perceived stakes for both contests made traditional small-scale quasi-deniable intervention impossible.

For the United States, since 1989 finding a substitute for war and all its complications is best accomplished, if at all possible, by intervention, that is, by a more measured (and often clandestine) application of force to an opponent, which may be a sovereign state or an elusive political or religious movement seen as a threat to American security. Here the philosophical principle is likely to be based on utilitarianism, a version of rational choice, as the most moral solution to a troubling problem of American foreign policy. Whether intervention at root is a moral solution preferable to war is an open question. Choosing which of these options should be used is the task of the statesman.

One should note in passing that a relatively new category of intervention (apart from the standard categories that will be discussed later) is terrorism. This is not to say that terrorism was invented only after World War II and highlighted, for example, the success of Israel in establishing itself as a state. In

Machiavelli's day, the poisoner and assassin in the employ of Cesare Borgia was a common weapon. The difference today is that states or groups with a grievance against America, rightly or wrongly perceived, make the use of terror tactics a continuing campaign for broad political decisions that they feel cannot be accomplished through other means. Such assaults are part of the price Americans must pay for not being able to satisfy the desire for autonomy, self-determination, or further prestige of each and every group that somehow is involved in our orbit. Someone's self-determination is the breakup of someone else's state.

When an existing state is supporting such programs, we refer to it as "state terrorism," whereas the less complex attacks on behalf of a charismatic leader of a religious or political cause are simply terrorism. To the victim, it is a distinction without a difference. To security organizations of the U.S. government, state terrorism has far more dangerous potential. Generally, terrorism is the weapon of the weak. The United States in particular is vulnerable because of its worldwide interests that are certain to offend someone on political or religious grounds, and the vast number of nationalities represented among the U.S. citizenry. Terrorism creates civic distrust and scapegoating and is a heavy but inevitable burden for all to bear. "Fighting fire with fire" is only a partial solution, although Jimmy Carter's speech at American University in 1979 proposing to fight communist fire with water did not seem feasible either.

An intermediate stop on the road to armed and open intervention is the covert military operation. Advocates of such operations, like William E. Colby, Central Intelligence Agency (CIA) director in the mid-1970s, believed that they added another arrow to the statesman's quiver. There might be a situation in which war or open intervention was impractical, yet doing nothing would be an offense to either our honor or our common sense.[1] The rationale for this kind of operation—in Guatemala, Indonesia, Iran, and so on—is "plausible denial." But the targets are seldom fooled by the question of agency. In any case, in the heyday of the Reagan administration and the Reagan Doctrine, the support of "freedom fighters" anywhere was government policy.

Turning again to traditional intervention, we find a wide number of categories short of armed intervention. For intervention that is a violation of a sovereign nation's autonomy, a subjecting of its will to an outside force, there are some subtle and some not-so-subtle methods. Many of these are covert in nature, the realm of the CIA. Propaganda and disinformation aimed at discredit-

---

1. See Evan Thomas, *The Very Best Men: Four Who Dared* (New York: Simon & Schuster, 1995), for CIA "covert operations" from 1947 to 1961.

ing the political leadership, for example, are commonplace. Forgeries and faked photos fall into this category. Use of the spiritual descendants of Machiavelli's poisoners and assassins was specifically prohibited by law after the Cuban Bay of Pigs incident. Economic sabotage, counterfeit currency, and the like also fall into this category of covert operation.[2]

We have already covered the situation in regard to war. Two particular points were stressed: under international law, all countries have an equal right as sovereign states to decide to go to war; and most states tend to invoke just war criteria in support of that decision, to placate both domestic and international opinion. Since the end of the Cold War, there have in fact been few declared wars; rather, the trend has been toward "intervention."

One does not have to go far to find the reasons for this trend. A formal declaration of war has many legal implications, everything from considerations of blockades and the freedom of the seas to whether your Lloyd's of London policies will be valid. Further, there is the question (especially for small states) of stirrings from the UN or perhaps a major power taking exception to the action. To settle unresolved differences by intervention avoids some of these problems and seems to have either the approval or the blind eye of the international community.

How could it be that the use of force under one banner is acceptable while the identical action under the banner of war meets with general opprobrium? This certainly was not the original intention. The Treaty of Westphalia in 1648 was designed to preserve the territorial status quo in Europe. One of the requirements that had to be observed if this order was to be preserved was the principle of nonintervention. To preserve the fiction dear to international lawyers of the equality of states, every state was equally sovereign inside its own territory. There it could do as it chose; the relationship between the state and its citizens was nobody else's business. The equal right of all to declare war with perfect legality was part of this fiction.

In the history of Europe since the seventeenth century, the violation of the integrity of one state by another has not been infrequent, but the principle continued to endure and is reflected in the charter of the UN, with the possible exception of genocide as an international concern. Yet in the current international climate, the preference for intervention or in any case some action short of declaring war is the new, imperfect norm. After reviewing the recent history, we will consider Panama, Somalia, Bosnia, and the Persian Gulf—all involving the

---

2. See ibid., 209–10, 305–10, for examples of attempts to assassinate Castro.

United States, with its rich history of intervention—to see in the end what the rationale was and how the legacy of historical realism figures in these events.

In our consideration of the just war theory, emphasis was placed on the ecclesiastical background in putting into place certain rules of convenience and prudence, with moral overtones, that set the conditions for going to war, if one wanted to advance under the flag of justice. States engaged in "intervention" sometimes evoke the same justification as the just war rules—to right a wrong—and claim to pay strict attention to proportionality of violence and double effect, the safeguarding of the civilian population, and so on. Yet there are no fixed criteria for intervention that carry the same weight as the time-tested just war criteria. Brian Hehir, a Jesuit scholar who served as secretary for the Catholic bishops in their labor over the morality of nuclear weapons, has turned his attention to intervention, seeking, as he puts it, an "ethic of intervention."[3]

Hehir correctly notes the enormous change in world appreciation of the balance of power with the end of the bipolar world. He agrees with Kissinger's *Diplomacy* that a multipolar world is already in existence and that power is not simply one-dimensional military power but rather diverse and different forms encompassing economics and culture and, as we shall see in the next chapter, the power exhibited by such issues and their supporters as the environment and human rights. As Hehir sees it, the two principles now under attack in the post–Cold War world are exactly the two pillars of Westphalia, the sovereignty of states and the norm of nonintervention.[4] The interconnectedness of the modern world has blurred traditional sovereignty, for example, and given it a new relativity.

Adding to the urgency of locating and defining an "ethic of intervention" has been the dramatic shift in opportunities for intervention by those powers with the intention and means to do so. During the Cold War, in the bipolar context, intervening in another state's affairs might pose a severe risk if the rival saw it as in any way threatening the power balance, in actuality or even symbolically. For example, during the decades when Somalia was referred to as the "Horn of Africa" and allegedly controlled the sea lanes to the Middle East oil, the idea of one or the other great powers (that is, the United States or the Soviet Union) lightly intervening was unthinkable. The beneficiaries of this system by and large were Third World countries, courted by both sides, and in this process

---

3. See Brian Hehir, "Intervention: From Theories to Cases," *Ethics and International Affairs* 9 (1995): 1–14.

4. Ibid., 2.

laying some claim to a kind of aid and comfort that has been denied them since the end of this particular confrontation.

Now, in the increasingly interdependent world, there are likely to be more rather than fewer occasions for one nation to intervene in the affairs of another precisely because of this overlap of interest. True, the interdependence may well lead to more friendly and peaceful relationships, but one should not ignore this other likely and dangerous possibility. As Hehir puts it, the struggle is likely to be between order and justice, an almost certain recipe for trouble. Hehir summarizes this argument as follows: "A singular characteristic of international politics in the 1990's is the way in which both the empirical character of state behavior and the norms governing world politics have combined to increase the scope of interventionary activity and to raise the question of whether a change in the normative view of intervention is needed today. Neither a purely political nor a purely ethical argument will be sufficient to respond to this question."[5]

The reason for this is clear from our earlier discussion, for example, of Machiavelli and later of the just war tradition. For Machiavelli, the question of whether to intervene was a simple case of *necessito*. If the prince decided that intervention was required, the question that remained was one of means: did he have the resources, mainly military, to carry out this affair of state? If so, his concern then became consequential: would the gain justify the risk? These considerations are not unlike the contemporary problem. Modern rulers may perhaps have to pay more attention to the "ethical" argument in this sense: if the intervention is seen as simple aggression, and unless the intervenor is one of the members of the Security Council, there may be an international response based on the UN Charter, which might undo or at least complicate the joys of intervention. The matter of the disapproval of the world community is not entirely ineffective if it extends to trade sanctions or embargo. But Hehir is correct in noting that in this era coming up with an international standard to judge intervention to replace the old Westphalian norm of nonintervention is no simple matter. One can see that a variety of standards are in operation today; reviewing the U.S. historical position on intervention provides some detail against which new conclusions might be drawn.

It can be argued that international intervention in the post–Cold War world poses unique problems, especially for the United States, which has created, carried out, and promoted a variety of standards in line with its national purpose, as interpreted by a variety of leaders. An earlier American belief about intervention was expressed in the Monroe Doctrine of 1823, warning Europe to abide by

5. Ibid., 5.

Westphalia, excluding only itself from that restriction in regard to Latin America. After World War II, the user-friendly formula was anticommunism in selected areas to avoid unsettling the Russian bear. All the often large-scale interventions by American military forces and their allies were in regions peripheral to the great power struggle: intervention in Africa and Asia, for example, since the 1960s were carried out under that banner—the Congo, Ethiopia, Eritrea, Indonesia, Vietnam, and so on were all done under that slogan. The empirical marginality of these encounters in no way lessened their enthusiastic pursuit or symbolic importance, if no other reason amenable to the logic of historical realism was available.

After the end of the Cold War in 1989, with no perceived military threat (although nuclear weapons and missiles still bristled in China and Russia), the United States needed to rethink the sufficient and necessary conditions for intervening so readily in the affairs of other nations. The interdependency of the world was one option, but as the leading military power, the United States did not wish to cash in its best chip altogether. Still, reasons were now more urgently needed to explain those moves both to the American public and to the world at large. The new age of political contingency has opened up the whole field, particularly so because the easy justification of Machiavelli's day is not feasible. The moral choice must be a convincing one. As Zbigniew Brzezinski put it in his 1993 book *Out of Control*, the final point of the realist paradigm, morality, was redundant in the age of communism; now in the time of contingency, he says, moral choice and ethical consideration must be included in our political and military calculations.[6] So again, intervention causes a crisis in decision making, especially in the cases of Bosnia and the Persian Gulf.

For one thing, the United States always feels a tension between global responsibilities and national interests. Sometimes there may be a perfect fit (say World War II), but usually not. We will review four different instances of intervention, namely, Panama and its aftermath, Somalia and its antinomies, and, most difficult of all, the fate of the former Yugoslavia and the issue of Iraq. National interest, defined in terms of power, is often harder to define today than yesterday but nonetheless must be the goal. This goal must meet the national interest standard; otherwise, it cannot be articulated, and a goal that defies articulation cannot expect to muster political support at home or abroad. This is the rock-bottom justification for intervention.

The immediate problem stems from bringing in the just war tradition and trying to apply it to intervention. The issue is the use of force, which, ideally,

6. Zbigniew Brzezinski, *Out of Control* (New York: Collier, 1996).

under the just war theory, had to do with promoting justice. This could be done, however, only under the umbrella of Europe and the Catholic Church in medieval times, which provided a community of law and morality that was the norm of the day. Moving these standards into an altogether different world is bound to be unsuccessful, although attention is still paid to the old (failed) model of the just war. There are similarities in the current American domestic scene when some argue that the mores and norms of today somehow should be like those in the days of the founding fathers, without analyzing the amazing (and sometimes regrettable) change in the conditions of ordinary life then and now. Not burdened by the legal restrictions and traditions of actually declaring war, the ruler intent on intervention can always claim some version of justice for his own side, which will be verified or faulted depending on the outcome of his adventure. This seems to be the norm of the moment.

In partial answer to those who promote the legitimacy of claims for justice as an excuse for intervention, there are those who argue against intervention, and their arguments must be considered and overcome if the would-be intervenor is to carry the day. The critics raise three points. First is the risk of escalation into nuclear war, the classical Cold War model. This risk still exists, and each intervention raises that possibility. To the extent that interventions are near the edge of China's interests, they are among the more risky. But America still likes to flex its muscles over Taiwan's integrity, Chinese human rights, and intellectual property rights. Second is whether intervention will impede the formation of a stable international order. Whatever the injustices built into the Westphalian system, the appearance and usually the fact of order were highly valued. An issue like Kuwait in 1990 aroused the international community; a majority of the UN states were similarly vulnerable to a takeover by *force majeur* and were avid supporters of the idea of rollback. This indeed occurred, but probably not so much to preserve the international order (although surely that was a factor) but because of the importance of a reliable international oil order. There is no question that the sanctity of states is a force for order although, it can be equally argued, not necessarily a force for justice. Here again is the need for diplomacy and compromise so that every disagreement, every issue, is not a question of war or peace, intervention or nonintervention. Third is the question of whether intervention will abrogate the responsibility of peoples to resolve their own problems. Here we see the hand of Immanuel Kant, who realized that a key ingredient for a national state was the development of the people who lived there. Kant, however, was thinking primarily of a European-style state, where a predominant majority founded a state on blood, language, religion, and common mores and customs. To some extent, the fragmentation of larger states fits into this category, allowing for the creation of new miniature arrivals. But this makes no easier the task for the multinational and multicultural states that somehow will have to carry the burden for whatever international community finally expresses itself out of the intellectual rubble of the end of the Cold War.

Over the past decade, several of our political leaders have dealt directly with the problem of intervention and the use of force, leading to our present dilemma. Former secretary of defense Caspar Weinberger set up six conditions for the deployment of U.S. forces in a 1984 speech: the United States should not commit forces to combat overseas (war or intervention) unless the particular engagement or occasion is deemed vital to U.S. national interest; the commitment should be made only "with clear intention of winning"; it should be carried out with "clearly defined political and military objectives"; it must be "continually reassessed and adjusted if necessary"; it should "have the support of the American people and their elected representatives in Congress"; and it should be a "last resort."

This six-point statement clearly reflects the Pentagon's Vietnam experience, which it was at considerable pains not to repeat. Still, it was not without its critics. Secretary of State George P. Shultz denounced these conditions as the "Bomb Moscow syndrome." In other words, with this stack of conditions, it was difficult to imagine under what circumstances America's armed forces might be ready to participate in the implementation of U.S. policy. In brief, who is in charge here? Defense presumably is a servant of the president and secretary of state. These conditions, however, in the context of the time, were perhaps not so unreasonable as they sound today, especially in regard to the chain of command. Further, almost any move in the zero-sum anticommunist game might lead to more uncontrollable escalation. When we worried about the strategic significance of the Horn of Africa, for example, the December 1992 "humanitarian intervention" in Somalia would have been unthinkable.

The question of intervention continued to attract the highest level of consideration and introspection. In the final days of his administration, George Bush turned his attention to the same problem, that is, under what conditions America should be prepared to use force. He tied the idea first to leadership. "Leadership, well, it takes many forms. It can be political or diplomatic, it can be economic or military, it can be moral or spiritual leadership. Leadership can take any one of these forms or it can be a combination of them. Leadership should not be confused with either unilateralism or universalism. We need not respond by ourselves to each and every outrage of violence. The fact that America can act does not mean that it must." (This seems to resolve the dilemma that some raise over Kantian ethics: that ought implies can and can implies should.) Bush saw creating a specific list of rules as a "futile quest," but nonetheless he favored some guidelines. His effort was characteristically imprecise. "Using military force makes sense as a policy where the stakes warrant, where and when force can be effective, where no other policies are likely to prove effective, where its application can be limited in scope and time, and where the potential benefits justify the potential costs and sacrifice. Once we are satisfied that force makes sense, we must act with the maximum possible support. The United States can and should lead, but we will want to act in concert, where possible, involving the United Nations or other multinational grouping." Bush concluded his ruminations on this subject: "But in every case involving the use of force, it will be essential to have a clear and achievable mission, a realistic plan for accomplishing the mission, and criteria no less realistic for withdrawing US forces once the mission is complete. Only if we keep these principles in mind will the potential sacrifice be one that can be explained and justified."[7]

While these guidelines seemed sound and prudential from January through March 1993, by April, Secretary of State Warren Christopher, under considerable harassment over Bosnia, delivered another guide for the perplexed. First, he said, the goal must be clearly stated; second, there must be a strong likelihood of success; third, there must be an "exit strategy"; and fourth, the action must win sustained public support. Such a formula places a great deal of weight on the first point because the other three are completely unknowable. None of these forays, to be sure, settles any major question on the justification of the use of force or intervention into other people's affairs. They are indicative, however, of the unsettled nature of the subject.

The example of Panama in December 1989 might best be described as a category of American intervention, Central and Latin American style, more typical of the nineteenth century. Those were the days when considerations of state sovereignty were most easily laid aside by North Americans, that is, the United States. Because fifteen thousand American troops were already in Panama under previous treaty arrangements, the actual intervention was relatively simple and the end never in doubt. By the time another thirteen thousand American troops were put into the equation, as well as Stealth bombers, the only concern was to try to minimize civilian casualties. Even then three hundred or more Panamanians were killed in the melee and the Panama Defense Forces surrendered. President Manuel Noriega was finally captured and then convicted in an American court on narcotics charges. One of his last public acts be-

---

7. *New York Times*, 6 January 1993.

fore the intervention was to wave an old sword and personally declare war on the United States. No one took this threat seriously, but it was added to the list of Panamanian offenses. Panama was the classic "might makes right" equation and "self-help" the only recourse for the Panamanians if they wished to contest the American intervention. This adventure demonstrated above all the classic notion of an inherent American right to work its will in the Western Hemisphere, the Monroe Doctrine updated. In 1904 President William Howard Taft had made what may be the ultimate statement of American confidence. Taft said that soon there would be three American flags equidistant in the hemisphere: one at the North Pole, one in Panama, and one at the South Pole, demonstrating that by "moral superiority of race" it all belonged to the United States.

There is not much new for us to learn from the case of Panama, but it is worth considering because it provides a contrast with the next two cases, which show different facets of the intervention phenomenon. Somalia represents a whole new order of intervention, which, if it sets a precedent, would open almost unlimited new possibilities. Somalia has a long history, including more than one hundred years of colonialism, when it changed hands periodically among the British, Italians, Ethiopians, and French. During this period of lusty imperialism, the practice of taking what countries were available on the basis of superior force was commonplace. Through these practices, the great powers cut up what geography they could and those left unsatisfied threatened war. Germany's late entry into this game was one of the causes of German dissatisfaction that helped to ignite World War I.

In the 1960s Somalia was given its independence but fell under the tyranny of its own competing elites. "The Somali conflict is essentially a contest among Somali elites over the most coveted of all national institutions, the state. However, this intraclass struggle is interfaced with clannish loyalties. Such a complication renders the construction of a national front elusive. Somalia approaches the end of the twentieth century with few friends, while it descends deeper into fragmentation, general pauperism, and mutual predacity." This brief description of the root of Somalia's problem is in the *The Oxford Companion to Politics of the World,* so one must assume that such information is readily available to any interested party.[8] Yet, in December 1992, about three years after deciding it was necessary to punish Panama, the Bush administration, almost as a beau geste at the end of the term, decided to answer the call of suffering humanity

---

8. Joel Krieger, ed., *The Oxford Companion to Politics of the World* (New York: Oxford University Press, 1993), 845.

and relieve the ghastly starvation in Somalia. That this situation was both self-inflicted and the result of a recurring natural cause—drought—did not detract from the supposed nobility of the mission. All that was required was twenty-eight thousand American troops and food supplies, the most straightforward of plans. The Bush administration's assumption was that the troops would return a month later, in time for the inaugural, and after an expenditure of only $300 million. Once the U.S. force arrived—soon to be bolstered by various UN units—the political fragmentation described in the *Oxford Companion* became apparent and coalition-building attempts were replaced by a policy aimed at disarming the warring Somalian factions.

With no easy end in sight, the United States, in its capacity as a permanent member of the UN Security Council, turned the whole operation over to the UN, unaware of or unconcerned about the possibility of other agendas arising once the Security Council vote was taken and the UN bureaucracy took over the administration of this so-called humanitarian relief effort. Soon the mission was expanded to nation building with all its complications and expense—actually substantial aid under the guise of food relief. The peacekeeping budget was increased to $1.5 billion. (The Ford Foundation released a report chaired by the American Paul Volker and the Japanese Sadako Ogata with ideas on how to finance peacekeeping operations, but so far, no report, official or private, has explained how to reconstruct failed states.) Therefore, the Somalian operation continued. Casualties mounted among the Somalians and Americans and UN units alike. The UN Security Council in September 1993 voted to end the operation no later than March 1995. For the Americans, the next spring was late enough.

Does one learn anything from these egregious forays into the world of hunger and famine and need? Is intervention, no matter what its purpose and motivation, always at risk of doing more harm than good? One wonders whether the United States followed any of the stated guidelines for dispatching troops overseas and whether the UN was the proper instrument for this activity. One needs to consider in this connection the American experience in orchestrating the Gulf War against Iraq in 1991.

There were two grand stages, the preparation for the war, dubbed Desert Shield, and then the actual war itself, Desert Storm. The preliminary activities were also in two stages: getting approval from the United Nations Security Council, where the Chinese and Soviets were only lukewarm (agreement was reached to liberate Kuwait and roll back to the original borders, but the mandate did not extend beyond that), and getting congressional approval. The War Powers Act passed by Congress during the Nixon administration was designed narrowly to end the Vietnam War but, more broadly, to be certain that Congress had the power of war and peace. Nixon vetoed the act as unconstitutional, but it passed anyway. The constitutionality of this act has never been brought before the Supreme Court. Bush's advisers recommended he bypass Congress once the UN resolution was in hand; but Bush won over Congress, the constitutional issue still unresolved.[9]

So the war was fought and Kuwait liberated, according to the UN mandate and the attitude and interest particularly of the Arab allies who participated, notably Saudi Arabia and Egypt. So the UN plan was achieved. But what about basic American interests? They ran far beyond the liberation of Kuwait but were not furthered. The job of the general is to win the battle; the job of the statesman is to convert the victory into lasting political benefits. This is a good example of the downside of multilateral action, when the intention and interest of the players clearly differ. The cost to the United States of the UN flag turned out to be very high. If the goal is simply to roll back, then the case for multilateralism can be made; if there is more at stake, the intervenor has to consider the differences and not simply paper them over in deference to some vague UN prestige. Thus the Iraq issue continued to fester.

Similar concerns arise over the UN's eagerness to find cases for peacekeeping. One requirement might be that a real peace actually exist before the "peacekeepers" are moved in. In the case of Somalia, the "mission creep" from humanitarian delivery of food soon escalated into a political and military operation designed to disarm miscreants, create political stability by supporting one side over the other, and finally to go into nation building, an idea floated without much success in the 1960s to help justify the Vietnam War. Worse, from the American perspective—which had no imperial or national interest in this program—was that much of the actual fighting and killing fell to the U.S. forces, especially the helicopter gunships. But there were also the daily realities reported in the media. For example, "United States troops today raided a building near Digler Hospital to search for mortar-firing tubes but did not find any. During the raid, a Somali woman lost both legs when the Americans blew open a wall to enter. Major Stockwell said the woman had ignored a loudspeaker warning to leave the building."[10]

Blame must be assessed on a humanitarian operation if the implementation is anything but that. Multilateral, or UN, involvement by definition complicates

9. For more details, see Robert J. Myers, "Ethics, Democracy and Foreign Policy: Manipulation or Participation?" *Philosophy* 13 (November–December 1991): 24–28.

10. *New York Times,* 20 September 1992.

the problem of responsibility. Once the UN Security Council has approved a course of action, no one seems to wish to step up and talk about the moral questions that soon arise. Who bears the moral weight of the outcomes of these antiseptic resolutions? When everyone is responsible, no one is responsible. Has the bureaucracy of the UN become the actor rather than the creature of the Security Council? The levity shown by some UN bureaucrats is not reassuring. The undersecretary general for peacekeeping (who has spent his entire career in the UN) has stated: "Just look to where we've got to now. A force of heavily armed soldiers is keeping order and distributing food in Somalia . . . and another 25,000 armed soldiers are doing similar work in the former Yugoslavia" (before the United States entered that arena in December 1995).

It is worthwhile projecting from Chapter 7 the theory of how the UN is to work, the observations made by world leaders, pro and con, and then to see what happens in the field. While intervention by and large is unilateral and conducted by sufficiently motivated parties, one can see that under certain conditions, usually marginal to the primary intervenor, using the UN route and spreading the responsibility is attractive, as the Gulf War was to the United States. One can and should argue, however, that if the criteria established over a long historical time were used, the realism position on intervention appears to be the most satisfactory. Does the proposed intervention satisfy vital national interests, or is it relatively marginal, a question of prestige and pride, which, I have noted earlier, are sufficient motives for war? The hazards of intervention are many, both prudentially and morally, which suggests that such adventures be used with great caution and against clear-cut expectations.

As we have seen, the wisdom of Immanuel Kant was against intervention. A nation, he thought, provided the best possibility for developing the full capacities of nations and their citizens; and intervention (with those thoughts in mind) bore the heavy responsibility to be as certain as possible that it accomplish more good than harm. Nations with powerful armed forces, aspirations, and a capacity for self-deception are the most vulnerable to the temptations of intervention, ignoring at their peril the advice of the realist tradition.

9 The Environmental and Human Rights
Challenges to Realist Politics

In popular contemporary discussion of international relations, there is substantial consideration of the growing interdependence of the world. This is true, although in a restricted sense: financial markets, air travel, television, and radio—the money, media, and communications complex—certainly bring peoples in contact; but it may be going too far to assume that this necessarily represents an advance in a community of trust and interest. This interdependence may, on the contrary, have an opposite effect. This idea, as I have already pointed out, is a daily task of the United Nations. Integrative and centrifugal forces continue to be in play. In this context, two relatively new and important issues demand the attention of the realist as well as the idealist and for the usual divergent interests: the environment and human rights. These issues are inextricably interrelated and are divisive: Developed nations tend to uphold the attitudes of the West against large portions of the East as well as underdeveloped nations in general. These issues also pit authoritarians against democrats and spill over into other concerns of nations; they therefore raise the potential for international conflict and certainly interstate indignation. For those reasons, these issues are able to mobilize power and make their weight felt on the scale of relevant problems in the international community. A further complication for the environmental issue (insofar as it can be separated from human rights) is the new and perhaps bizarre turn it has taken into the realm of national security.

The explicit relationship between the environment and national security began with the publication of Al Gore's best-selling book *Earth in the Balance*, which not only dealt with traditional environmental issues such as air and water but proposed as a new "organizing principle" for the world—in the aftermath of communism, which had filled that role for the West—a dedication to the environment. The next great campaign, said then-senator Gore, should be based on the "organizing principle" of saving the earth and its inhabitants through timely and massive attention to the global environment.[1]

It was not until the advent of the Clinton-Gore administration that the connection between environment and security went from general notion to specific plan. In October 1995 the *New York Times* reported "the greening of American diplomacy," which added to the nation's intelligence responsibilities a list of new targets. The old familiar targets were massing of troops, development of weapons of mass destruction, the pecking order in the Kremlin, arms shipments to Cold War surrogates in the Third World, and so on, dealing with military power and the capabilities and intentions of foes. Now, in addition, the "intelligence community" is supposed to be aware of rainfall levels and water tables in order to anticipate famine and the collapse of governments; infant mortality rates, also an indicator of the stability of governments; high rates of population growth that might set off rebellion or ethnic strife; the enlargement of the Sahara Desert, which could cause new famine and strife; inflation rates and trade deficits, which also affect government stability; and the ability of Third World countries to absorb youth into the labor market.

A focus on different priorities was demonstrated by the Clinton administration in establishing a new position in the Department of State: undersecretary for global affairs. The undersecretary, Tim Wirth, said that the four chief concerns of the Department of State are population growth, climate changes, narcotics, and food scarcities.[2] This is all of one piece with the environmental concentration, but from a realist perspective, these are secondary to the priorities traditionally involved in national security.

No one can deny that such factors have an influence on the fortunes of nations, but some in October 1995 raised the question as to whether these data— easily accessible to anyone with an interest, some talent, and money for the looking or asking—should be assigned to people who require expensive security clearances and middle-class salaries. The new intelligence targeting brought along with it the official explanation. "During the cold war, most security threats stemmed from state-to-state aggression, so most of the analysis was of factors that could produce state-to-state aggression," according to James Steinberg, the Department of State's director of policy planning. "Now we're focusing more on internal factors that can destabilize governments and lead to civil wars and ethnic strife. Now we're paying much more attention to early warning

---

1. Al Gore, *Earth in the Balance: Ecology and the Human Spirit* (Boston: Houghton-Mifflin, 1992).

2. *Stanford Daily*, 14 October 1996, reporting on a Wirth speech at Stanford on 9 October.

factors, like famine and the environment." These concerns have led to considerable rethinking of intelligence requirements in the CIA, for example, which is
creating an annual study on "global humanitarian emergencies." One intelligence official explained: "We've been looking at some of these softer issues for
a long time. What's different now is that these issues have moved from the periphery to take a more central role."[3]

This seemingly seamless process in intelligence targeting and gathering has
not come to the fore without criticism. "All this stuff is a silly idea," said Angelo
Codevilla, an intelligence specialist who teaches at Boston University. "The
purpose of intelligence is to ferret out secrets from people who want to keep
those secrets. To turn intelligence into environmental reports is not to understand environmental problems or intelligence." He advocates staying with the
"hard targets" because "guns will determine the future of the world as they ever
did."[4]

There was a dissent from these claims by Toby Gatti, assistant secretary of
state for intelligence: "This soft stuff immediately becomes hard when you have
to send in the Marines." George Moose, assistant secretary of state for African
affairs, also supports this new environmental targeting, citing Somalia. One
suspects that the impetus for this work, emanating in the first instance from the
vice-president, may serve several bureaucratic purposes as well as some possible
good. CIA director John Deutch, in a speech before the World Affairs Council
in Los Angeles on 16 July 1996, added more details on the CIA's role in environmental matters. First, he establishes the importance of the environmental message for the washed and unwashed alike: "The environment is an important
part of the Intelligence Community agenda. . . . Environmental trends, both
natural and man-made, are among the underlying forces that affect a nation's
economy, its social stability, its behavior in world markets, and its attitude
toward neighbors."

One could argue that this approach is a long way around the barn, that a traditional well-placed secret agent at the shoulder of the traditional prime minister might be able to reveal information on these trends, more accurately and
with more insight than the sober gathering of such details by an analyst—
probably with no firsthand knowledge of the area in question—would ever
provide and, in all probability, much earlier. If multilateralism is in vogue in
matters of potential interventions, then it should follow that environmental in-

---

3. *New York Times*, 9 October 1995.
4. Ibid.

formation of intelligence value should also be gathered through these same methods and in the same spirit.

Deutch does not make the same mistake that some human rights advocates have made in insisting that one principle or concern is the whole of the matter, even though he hangs onto the environmental bone, as required, through his long speech. "I emphasize that environment is one factor. It would be foolish, for example, to attribute conflicts in Somalia, Ethiopia, or Haiti to environmental causes alone. It would be foolhardy, however, not to take into consideration that the land in each of these states is exploited in a manner that can no longer support growing populations." Another argument advanced for having an organization such as the CIA involved in promoting "environmental intelligence" is one of convenience and economy. Deutch explains: "National reconnaissance systems that track the movement of tanks through the desert, can, at the same time, track the movement of the desert itself, see the sand closing in on formerly productive fields or hillsides laid bare by deforestation and erosion. Satellite systems allow us to quickly assess the magnitude and severity of damage. Adding this environmental dimension to traditional political, economic, and military analysis advances our ability to alert policy makers to potential instability, conflict, or human disaster and to identify situations which may draw American involvement."

One possible criticism of this aim of Deutch's is that it seems to be seeking out things to do rather than concentrating on those many fewer situations—in which some environmental disaster may play a part—in which the criterion remains the realist one, namely, a meaningful definition of national interest, a vital concern that requires the attention of our vast national security apparatus. Deutch goes on, however, to claim the close involvement of the State Department, one of his principal clients: "Diplomacy will be ever more concerned with the global debate over environmental issues." As Secretary of State Warren Christopher said in April (in a speech on 9 April 1996 at Stanford University), "Our ability to advance our global interests is inextricably linked to how we manage the Earth's natural resources." He emphasized that we must put environment "in the mainstream of American foreign policy," as Deutch asserts he will do as he concludes his address.[5]

Linking the environment with intelligence in this way perhaps creates the suspicion evoked by a *New York Times* headline of 15 October 1995: "U.S. Will Deploy Its Spy Satellites on Nature Mission," with the byline, "A Huge Environmental Study Gives a New Lease on Life to Intelligence Systems." Since the

---

5. *Stanford Daily,* 10 April 1996.

beginning of warfare, the terrain, lay of the land, night and day, floods or fords, and so on have played a prominent part in military planning; and at its most benign, the new emphasis on "environmental intelligence" is nothing more than that. The issue itself, however, is politically loaded and therefore is difficult to present successfully as a new program justifying the use of expensive technology and people. If this is a new fact of national security, it can be accommodated easily enough in the realist paradigm. It is part of the power structure.

Environmentalism in the John Muir sense, however, may or may not have influence on a realist analysis. To the extent that it picks up support and a large following, such as the Greens could muster for a time in Germany, it is an element that must be reckoned with. The power factor, however, is not always recognized as environmentalists set about straightening out the world. For example, cooperative efforts between such countries as Japan and the United States have been marred by the essentially commercial and competitive nature of anti-pollution equipment and the insistence that such countries as China, heavily dependent on coal for energy, clean up pollution at a cost of 10 percent of the GDP.[6] Environmental concerns are certainly recognized as a significant factor in international politics, for the reasons given by Deutch as well as the conflict of interests arising from such issues as pollution and the use of finite resources like timber and water and oil. Questions regarding the environment bear differently on the various countries involved according to their stage of economic, political, and social growth.[7]

Nicaragua, for example, is undergoing the same deforestation process that has blighted Borneo, Thailand, and the Philippines, to name only a few Southeast Asian examples. Third Worlders always answer criticisms of their forestry policies, in talking to Americans, by reminding us of the fate of the forests of North America. One would hope that there is some increased appreciation of how dangerous deforestation is for everyone, but this argument falls on deaf ears. The Nicaraguans have sold vast tracts of forests to South Korean corporations, not a noticeably sensitive group, whose loggers are ready to cut. Protests are arising (too late) from the Indians of Awas Tingni, whose native lands are being sacrificed for payments to the government; the timber concession happened to overlap with Indian claims. The Nicaraguan in charge of national forests holds this position: "Nobody lives there. Until somebody shows me a

---

6. See, for example, Elizabeth Capanneli, *Environmental Challenges in the People's Republic of China* (Manila: Asian Development Bank, 1993).

7. See Andrew Hurrell and Kingsbury Benedict, eds., *The International Politics of the Environment* (Oxford: Clarendon Press, 1992), esp. Part III, "Power and Conflict of Interest."

title, that land is government land."[8] This is one way that environment and human rights become intertwined. There is no indication that this confrontation made the U.S. president's daily intelligence brief.

The role of the environment in U.S. policy, nonetheless, is not settled, and the argument between clean air and industry, so to speak, will continue. The Clinton administration tried to downplay any trade-off between a good environment and economic growth at the Kyoto conference in January 1998. In November 1996 in Beijing, for an earlier example, Secretary of State Warren Christopher said at a press briefing: "Our economic growth and well-being is also dependent upon responsibly managing our national resources. For the United States and China, choosing between economic growth and environmental protection is what President Clinton has called 'a false choice, an unnecessary choice.' Both are vitally important and mutually reinforcing."[9]

If the new emphasis on intelligence—renaming old concerns and painting them in bright colors—can add complexity to our thinking about both intelligence and the environment, a thorough appraisal of the human rights issue will demonstrate its many facets that must be considered vis-à-vis foreign policy considerations. When she was UN ambassador, the present secretary of state, Madeleine K. Albright gave a tough analysis of what human rights meant to her and presumably to the United States: "Because we live in a country that is democratic, trade-oriented, respectful of the law and possessed of a powerful military whose personnel are precious to us, we will do better and feel safer in an environment where our values are widely shared, markets are open, military clashes are constrained and those who run roughshod over the rights of others are brought to heel." She relates human rights to the administration's expansion of democracy and believes this effort is a rightful goal of the United States through the United Nations.[10] Americans are often concerned and confused as to whether the human rights question is being given too much—or not enough—attention in diplomacy. Given the nature of interest groups, it is not surprising that these internal clashes are not simple to resolve. There are several reasons for this. First, in the immediate postwar period with the strong support of UN delegate Eleanor Roosevelt, the matter seemed to have been settled. This was in 1948 when the Universal Declaration of Human Rights was passed by the

---

8. *New York Times,* 25 June 1996.

9. Excerpts from press briefing, 20 November 1996.

10. Ambassador Madeleine K. Albright, U.S. representative to the United Nations, "Symposium on Human Rights and the Lessons of the Holocaust," Senator Thomas J. Dodd Research Center, Storrs, Conn., 17 October 1995.

UN General Assembly in its functional capacity and as such became part of international law. At this historic moment there were about fifty members of the United Nations; this was before the end of colonialism, and the United Nations members shared enough values and beliefs that the declaration passed unanimously. That probably could not happen today. The declaration was cast in the most liberal image possible. Altogether, there are thirty articles and a preamble, which concludes that "a common understanding of these rights and freedoms is of the greatest importance for the full realization of this pledge."

The first article says, "All human beings are born free and equal in dignity and rights. They are endowed with reason and conscience and should act toward one another in a spirit of brotherhood." One can find little fault with this aspiration as a broad goal of the way the world might work. Access to law and fair treatment is desirable, but then it soon moves into areas that the communist states especially would have trouble with, such as Article 13. "Everyone has the right to freedom of movement and residence within the borders of each State." Article 16 says that everyone should have a right to marry and establish a family.

Articles 17 through 21 are in a bill of rights style. But by Article 23, one finds social contract ideas that are not only difficult to enforce but exceptionally difficult for most if not all states to follow. Article 23 says, "Everyone has the right to work, to free choice of employment, to just and favourable conditions of work, and to protection against unemployment." The first paragraph of Article 25 states, "Everyone has the right to a standard of living adequate for the health and well-being of himself and of his family, including food, clothing, housing and medical care, and necessary social services, and the right to security in the event of unemployment, sickness, disability, widowhood, old age or other lack of livelihood in circumstances beyond his control."

This declaration established a standard that no one could meet and claimed the right to a worldwide system of welfare and entitlements that has not been reached in Europe or the United States. A UN declaration of such sweeping claims and conditions did, however, establish the rule of finger-pointing by rival states, since anyone could be accused of human rights violations with impunity. Everyone recognized the potential in this declaration both for humanitarianism and for mischief. And it was thought to be a guarantee against any possible repetition of the genocide that occurred in Nazi Germany.

This declaration on human rights, then, even in the United States, or perhaps particularly in the United States, exceeded all reasonable expectations of being carried out. It probably did a great deal of damage as well, in the sense that it led peoples of the world to expect that their governments had a positive obligation to assume responsibilities for food, shelter, clothing, and education that were beyond anyone's ability to provide. Given this stack of expectations, it is perhaps not surprising that in general there was not much evocation of violation of human rights in the 1950s or even 1960s. When it became clear, however, that the issue of First Amendment–type human rights would make a first-class political weapon, it was put into play, particularly by the United States. Here again the declaration proved to be a document of great versatility.

If human rights ran into difficulty at the theoretical as well as the delivery level, one should also note the problems and opportunities that have arisen when the issue has been tied to real American foreign policy. First let us consider the case of the Carter administration, when human rights became an important element of foreign policy—some charged it was the only element of American foreign policy and based their critique on that point. The context of Carter's taking of office must be considered in analyzing why he so quickly took up this new and then-novel policy. He was first of all coming to power after Nixon and the Watergate scandal. He promised not to lie to anyone, a pledge that seems alien in modern politics. Since both Nixon and Kissinger were seen as men of *realpolitik* and the status quo, with no moral sense as required by realism, such a policy of conscience seemed a good thing in itself. The possibility of unfavorable consequences was downplayed. This, then, was an extraordinary development, for if we had to characterize American foreign policy (and realism as well) in a single phrase, we would have to choose a "policy of consequences." The likely consequences are the stuff of the process of choice.

Such a policy is similar to a policy of utilitarianism, in line with Bentham's phrase "the greatest good for the greatest number." A policy of consequences tries to maximize the morality of American foreign policy interests, a seeming must for the president and his men and equally supported by a majority of the public. But there also loomed the possibility, because of Carter as a person, that some variation of Kantianism would prevail. The human rights banner was raised in our diplomatic confrontation with Nicaragua. Instead of staying with Anastasio Somoza Garcia, Jr., and his seedy dictatorship, for military and economic reasons, Carter dumped him over violations of human rights; the result was that the Sandinistas came to power. This development was the basis for Jeanne Kirkpatrick's famous (but now discredited) distinction between authoritarian and totalitarian (communist) states. The first category she favored supporting unswervingly if they were pro-West while the second should be resolutely opposed. Authoritarian states, she asserted, could be changed, but not totalitarian ones. So much for slogans etched in stone.

Carter's particular foreign policy philosophy and lack of experience in this area were revealed in his 1977 inaugural address. "Our commitment to human rights must be absolute," he said. But by June 1977 in a commencement speech at the University of Notre Dame, he seemed to have been briefed by a closet realist: "For too many years, we have been willing to adopt the flawed and erroneous principles of our adversaries, sometimes abandoning our own values for theirs. We have fought fire with fire, never thinking that fire is better quenched with water." Through failure, he said, "we" have regained our principles and values and "regained our lost confidence."

"First, we have affirmed America's commitment to human rights as a fundamental tenet of our foreign policy. In ancestry, religion, color, place of origin and cultural background, we Americans are as diverse a nation as the world has ever seen. No common mystique of blood or soil unites us. What draws us together, perhaps more than anything else, is a belief in human freedom. We want the world to know that our Nation stands for more than financial prosperity." Then he returns to the lessons he had recently learned: "This does not mean that we can conduct our foreign policy by rigid moral maxims. We live in a world that is complex, imperfect and which will always be imperfect—a world that is complex and confused.

"I fully understand the limits of moral suasion. We have no illusions that changes will come easily or soon. But I also believe that it is a mistake to undervalue the power of words and ideas that words embody. In our own history, that power has ranged from Thomas Paine's 'Common Sense' to Martin Luther King Jr.'s 'I have a Dream.'"

Carter's sizing up and judging of Somoza for his violation of human rights, particularly those in the bill of rights category, attracted a good deal of criticism, especially from the realist camp. The problem here was that Carter was engaged in a one-note moral crusade because of his dedication to human rights, while ignoring American security and economic considerations, which, in the lexicon of foreign policy considerations, cannot be so simply brushed aside. Carter encountered this ambiguity in his policy toward Iran and the shah, straying from the principles of interest, power, and morality. These adventures made Carter an easy target for critics.

The most persistent and effective critic of Carter's human rights policy was Jeanne Kirkpatrick, but even her eloquence could not stop the Reagan administration from adding the rhetoric of human rights to its arsenal to supply the intellectual foundation to the Reagan Doctrine. Referring to Carter's policy, Kirkpatrick said that it was essential to distinguish between rhetoric and politics. Otherwise, ideas become "rationalizations" failing to connect reality and the institutions needed to make ideas concrete. Her complaint about the Universal

Declaration of Human Rights is similar to the above, that is, the proffered rights exceed what any society can produce. She asserts that "utopian expectations concerning the human condition are compounded then by a vague sense that Utopia is one's due; that citizenship in a perfect society is a reasonable expectation for real persons in real societies."[11] An opposite position was accepted by the promoters of the declaration, however: that ideals had to be promoted and established as normative goals if there was to be any possibility that national borders, sealing off populations from the scrutiny of the world, could be breached and finally eliminated.

The Kirkpatrick critique also encompassed the moral sphere, which Carter liked to consider his own. "The consequences of trying to base a human rights policy on private virtue is a failure. Where institutions are not constructed on the basis of human proclivities and habits, failure is the inevitable result. Human rights can be, should be, must be, will be, taken into account by US foreign policy, but we have had enough of rationalism and purism, of private virtues and public vices."[12]

The Reagan administration, anxious to further discredit Carter on moralism and human rights, publicly turned against the old policy. Secretary of State Alexander Haig in 1981 pointed to "limits" on how far we could change other peoples' cultures and then nominated as assistant secretary of state for human rights a well-known human rights opponent, Ernest LeFevre. His nomination was discarded in favor of Elliot Abrahms, who saw a great value for human rights in a different context. He saw that if those who were struggling against communism were defined as "freedom fighters," they should be supported not only on nationalist grounds but in terms of universal human rights. He too was able to say, not without irony, that "human rights is at the core of the Reagan foreign policy." Reagan was soon comfortable in this human rights mantle, making as he did the subversion of any communist state altogether legitimate in the name of freedom. Obviously, the Reagan Doctrine was selectively applied against small states that were vulnerable to subversion and intervention rather than the Soviet Union or China. It is worth mentioning, however, that the issue of human rights did play an important role in the downfall of the Soviet Union, through the Helsinki accords of 1973, which guaranteed the Soviet Union and its satellites in Europe their borders in exchange for human rights projects inside those countries. Here is a classic case of unexpected consequences.

The debate over human rights as a political question has been most dramati-

11. "U.S. Security Policy in Latin America," *Commentary*, January 1981.
12. Ibid.

cally displayed in recent time on an international scale at two international conferences, one in Vienna in 1993 and another in Bangkok in 1996. In the Vienna conference, the trend toward more than one standard on human rights came into focus, especially among Asian countries following the Chinese position; Secretary of State Christopher spoke up strongly for the universal standard, and that position carried the day. The movement toward exceptionalism, however, was reinforced at the Bangkok conference, and the United States, in caving in on human rights in 1996 when dealing with China on trade issues, has further weakened the strength of human rights arguments as trump cards in diplomatic negotiations. This is not a simple black-and-white argument as proponents on either side would have one believe, especially since it has become a stumbling block in Chinese-American relations, now that China and the United States seem to be headed toward the next bipolar rivalry (weakening trends that some have noted toward a more multilateral international system).

The question of human rights in China is complicated by the long historical continuity in that country and by the coming to power of Chinese communism in the last fifty years. The rulers of the Chou dynasty (1122 B.C. to 751 B.C.) said that the dynasty existed for the sake of the people. Confucius (551–479 B.C.) and his principal disciple, Mencius, developed the philosophy of Confucianism, which supported the individual acting in harmony with his compatriots and honoring the emperor and the will of Heaven. The thrust of Confucian philosophy was oriented toward the individual and his efforts, through education, to enlighten himself and perform as a rational being in society.

Nonetheless, there is more than one definition of human rights, and this has brought the Chinese and Americans to cross purposes, in large part because of the addition of the communist element (where the individual exists and finds meaning only as part of the state) as well as a misunderstanding of modern Chinese reasoning (communism to one side) that exists today. One definition of human rights demonstrates the familiar dichotomy between "civil libertarian" or American First Amendment rights and "social and economic rights," the former the property of the West and the latter the property of the communists and socialists. There is the illusion that there are no more communist states, but one certainly must include China and its quarter of the world's population, even if one chooses to ignore North Korea, Vietnam, and Cuba. This distinction is nonetheless not as important as it once was; from the articles of the Universal Declaration of Human Rights quoted above, one can see that both these ideas are contained in the same package. There is also some convergence in how the world looks at human rights. The empirical facts seem to be that every country should at least respect those rights that do not require heavy capital investment, including freedom of expression, religion, association, humane treatment, and nonarbitrary arrest and imprisonment. If these rights are violated, one can expect to find human rights activists.

In a paper published in the *Frankfurter Allgemeine Zeitung* on 29 December 1993, Thomas Metzger, a leading American sinologist at the Hoover Institution, explained the Chinese perspective on human rights. Metzger quickly concedes China's "terrible record" on human rights but goes on to suggest, from his study of Chinese intellectual thought, that the Chinese (even with communism) are not alien to the idea of "universal" human rights (sanctioned by extragovernmental authority) as the current debate might indicate. His argument is clear as well as controversial. First, he claims that "paradoxically enough, it is a Western, not a Chinese, intellectual trend that has questioned the idea of reason as a universal moral standard and of natural law." "Leading Western philosophers," he writes, "like Alasdair MacIntyre doubt that there are universal human rights and prefer to speak of norms and laws reflecting different historical, cultural, and political traditions."[13] This is in fact the position MacIntyre takes in his book *After Virtue.*[14] He deplores the lack of classical cultural (Platonic) standards in American life, maintains everyone has his own philosophy or, perhaps more properly, point of view, based on "emotivism," his own interpretation of the world, and that the world is now being run by barbarians with no knowledge of the ancient virtues associated with good government and self-realization. Whether this opaque book indeed had a widespread impact on people's views may be subject to argument, but it does catch the essence of the United States as a relativist nation, a charge from the right. (This reinforces Metzger's point that Americans by and large do not proceed into the world from a declaration of universal values, even though a number do exist, such as our argument for the universal utility of political realism.)

The real issue at the moment, Metzger correctly says, "is a certain extreme Western emphasis on individual autonomy and ethical skepticism, the idea that, except for equality and individual freedom, there are no universal moral values which all individuals should respect. For most Chinese, liberals as well as Marxists, this is unacceptable. They believe that there are universally objective, rational moral standards, and that these should be used to set the parameters of freedom." This insight opens new vistas to contemplate the Chinese reaction to

13. Thomas A. Metzger, "Chinese Perspective on Human Rights," *Frankfurter Allgemeine Zeitung,* 29 December 1993, sourcing the *New York Times,* 20 June 1993.

14. Alasdair MacIntyre, *After Virtue: A Study in Moral Theory* (Notre Dame: Notre Dame University Press, 1981).

the West and its ideas of human rights, which should be factored into the debate. Metzger concedes, however, that "many scholars hold that Chinese culture goes too far the other way, tending toward collectivism and lacking any serious respect for the dignity and autonomy of the individual."[15]

The Chinese rejection of the Western version of human rights is not unrelated to the slow (but not inevitable) progress of China toward some form of democratic society. Local elections, relatively free markets, and expression and behavior that do not threaten the stability of the state fit into what is allowable by the state. It is possible that China will prove to be the last country in the world to resist "human rights" and its co-conspirator, democracy. Hegel's grand notion of the inevitable spread of democracy everywhere, thus bringing about the "end of history" (in the sense that then no more such development is possible), is still being tested in China. For some the possibility of turning back the liberal democratic wave may be more of a tactical gain than a "historical certainty." The weakness of Hegel lies in the possibility that such historically dependent arguments may fail as precipitously as did communism, also based on the philosophy of Hegel, as interpreted by Marx. Until the Chinese finally embraced Marx and Lenin in 1949, the idea of historical progress and the unfolding of history toward some purpose never entered the Chinese mind. They saw history as endless cycles, as did the Greeks, with waxing and waning empires as the determining historical pattern.

The current debate over the universality of human nature has been intensified by the addition of more Asian voices asserting the special character of their own culture and their exceptional treatment of liberal human rights. The Westphalian right of state sovereignty is invoked against the (largely toothless) sanctions available to the UN. Cases that readily come to mind are Malaysia (in part over its treatment of the Chinese minority), Indonesia (over its handling of East Timor), and Singapore (championing the community). According to Singapore's foreign minister Wong Kan Seng, "Too much stress on individual rights over the rights of the community will retard progress." Further, in some countries, he charges, "the community's interests are sacrificed because of human rights of drug consumers and traffickers."[16]

A look at the Bangkok conference in March 1996, attended by seventeen members of the European Union and seven members of the Association of Southeast Asian Nations plus leaders of China, Japan, and South Korea, is informative relative to this debate. The two groups decided, after much negotia-

---

15. Metzger, "Chinese Perspective on Human Rights."
16. Ibid.

tion, that the conference, primarily aimed at economics and trade, would not consider issues of human rights. The "clash of cultures" on a small scale thus verified Samuel Huntington's thesis in his *Foreign Affairs* article of summer 1993, later expanded into his book *The Clash of Civilizations and the Remaking of World Order.*[17]

The issue is succinctly stated in the l March 1996 edition of the *New York Times:* "Western governments argue that questions like labor standards, the environment and political freedoms are inseparable from economic shop talk, while many of their host [Asian] nations insist that there is an 'Asian way' that puts group welfare and rapid development first." Actual debate was avoided by the expedient of all participants reiterating their commitment to the United Nations Charter and the Universal Declaration of Human Rights.

Assaults on the environment and child labor, for example, part of the pattern of Asian economic success, were justified by some delegates and observers as being necessary if Asian governments were to live up to the developmental expectations of the rising middle class, which had to be placated if the ruling oligarchs were to sleep securely in their positions of power. And they were simply patterning this development on the rampant consumerism that has characterized the West. A Thai human rights supporter, commenting on the Bangkok meeting, said: "Actually, [the Asian participants] are the ones who are importing their development policies from the West, consumerism, capitalism, investment, industrialization. Human rights violations in this country [Thailand] are a by-product of that development, environmental problems, deforestation, the displacement of people, the gap between rich and poor." At least one objective of the conference was accomplished: confrontation was avoided. Leon Britain, a commission vice-president, said: "For some countries the choice may be between child labor and child starvation. But as they develop, they get to a point where it's reasonable to say, you've got to stop now."[18]

So for this particular conference, sufficient to the day was the evil thereof. Jack Donnelly, author of *Universal Human Rights in Theory and Practice,* emphasizes the need for a balanced human rights approach that relies on national efforts as well as international cooperation: "We should not stop analyzing the international dimensions of human rights, let alone give up pursuing human rights goals in national foreign policies and through international and regional regimes. But we must not forget that international mechanisms are at best sup-

---

17. Samuel P. Huntington, *The Clash of Civilizations and the Remaking of World Order* (New York: Simon & Schuster, 1996).

18. *New York Times,* 1 March 1996.

plemental to national endeavors. Furthermore, even specialists in international relations cannot successfully carry out studies of human rights independent of the work of students of national or comparative politics; even when the focus of our work is on the international dimension of human rights, we must pay greater attention to the interaction of national and international factors in the success or failure of international initiatives. International factors are but a small and subsidiary part of the picture."[19]

For the United States today, the human rights question continues to pose problems for a realist foreign policy, just as it did in the days of the Carter administration. But realism nowadays is willing to run more risks in being certain to include human rights considerations in foreign policy in order to be true to its formula of interest, power, and morality. My remaining task, now, is to relate what we have discussed in the narrative of this work thus far to what lies ahead for American foreign policy in the new millennium, in terms of the realist paradigm.

19. Jack Donnelly, *Universal Human Rights in Theory and Practice* (Ithaca: Cornell University Press, 1989), 269.

10   Looking to the Future: The United States and the Promise of Realism

Having now analyzed in a general way the principles of the conduct of international relations through the past two thousand years and concluded with an update on the state of the world in terms of contemporary concerns, we now come to a consideration of what is ahead. Is there anything beyond "more of the same"?

The end of the Cold War brought with it in many circles, especially in the United States, the expectation that somehow a "new international order," a phrase from then-president George Bush, was about to come into being. This notion was to confuse the end of the bipolar power system, Churchill's "two scorpions in the bottle" era, with a fundamental shift from the realist paradigm. Certainly there would be differences in the way the international world worked, but not fundamental ones. "Different" was probably a more accurate description than "new" order, implying vast and uncertain changes in the international firmament. As George Shultz, former secretary of state, put it, "No doubt the way the world works has changed permanently and dramatically. Yet when it comes to diplomacy many key attributes remain."[1]

Samuel P. Huntington writes, "World politics is entering a new phase, and intellectuals have not hesitated to proliferate versions of what it will be—the end of history, the return of traditional rivalries between nation states, and the decline of the nation state from the conflicting pulls of tribalism and globalism, among others. Each of these visions catches aspects of the emerging reality." The reality for Huntington is the conflict between the world's civilizations, a point to which we shall return.[2]

---

1. U.S. Institute of Peace, *Peaceworks* 18 (September 1997), republished in adaptation in Hoover Institution *Viewpoints*, No. 30-97.

2. Samuel P. Huntington, "The Clash of Civilizations?" *Foreign Affairs* 72 (Summer 1993): 89–93.

There is no gainsaying that the end of the Cold War in its most familiar form surely was a significant event and that such happenings as the tearing down of the Berlin Wall followed by the reunification of Germany, and the breakup of the former Soviet Union into republics, changed the prospects of the putative battlefield to one of more pastoral hue. But at the same time, statesmen were aware that international politics existed before the Cold War, during the Cold War, and after the Cold War, and that the wisdom of realism had been largely followed during the whole of the twentieth century, usually for the better, sometimes for the worse. (Iraq comes to mind as an example where realism was ignored.) The idea of newness and the need for "something else" seized some observers of the international scene. John Lewis Gaddis, for example, in a 1992 article in the *Chronicle of Higher Education,* launched an attack on the writings of Hans J. Morgenthau and other realists on the grounds that they had failed to predict the end of the Cold War.[3] For those who prefer crystal balls to reality, this criticism was well taken. But realist theory's levels of prediction are limited; they tend to follow the range set by Machiavelli in his inductive method. Because of its reliance on self-interest and the quest for power, realism places the statesman in the arena of decision making, forcing him thereby to exercise moral choice. Such choice may be based, as history reflects, on courage, expediency, or principle, but certainly on some notion of consequences, including moral outcomes. It is also dependent on the relationship between the relative power of the state system and the condition of the world community.

The actions of the USSR and the United States and its allies during the transformation of Soviet power into centrifugal units were fully within the realist tradition, each side weighing the balance of power in the new empirical situation and so far resolving most of those new dynamics in a peaceful manner. Those who really expect to have the future revealed to them have the option of the quantifiers, the rational choice movement, or futurologist groups. As I have pointed out, those who wish to anticipate the future tend toward the linear interpretation of history, which would include the above groups plus the dialecticians and the promoters of progress. The position of Karl Popper, however, in his espousal of antihistoricism, denies that there are any historical processes leading to predetermined ends. That criticisms still arise over the conduct of international politics should come as no surprise, for in the competition for prestige and power and gain, whether it is in domestic life or on the international scene, there are winners and losers, which creates a natural arena for complaint.

---

3. John Lewis Gaddis, "The Cold War's End Dramatizes the Failure of Political Theory," *Chronicle of Higher Education,* 22 July 1992.

In the Introduction, I pointed out that Morgenthau, as the father of twentieth-century realism, doubted that his six principles of international relations would be widely accepted as a workable theory because, as he put it, of the "general depreciation of power among the public at large." The three principles that I have extracted as perennial, namely, interest, power, and morality, still are the dominant measures of the soundness of policy. Why is it that there remains a genuine, but feckless, attempt on the part of the idealists and their neocolleagues to find a better way, in spite of the utility, success, and long historical continuity of the realist position? Is the lure of idealism irresistible?

Here again, the classical criticism of realism was laid down about six decades ago by E. H. Carr, one of the early twentieth-century advocates of realism, in reporting on the twenty-year crisis in Europe between World War I and World War II. He wrote in praise of realism that "only when the sham has been demolished [can there] be any hope of raising a more solid structure in its place." Yet he claims that the realist position is ultimately untenable. "Consistent realism excludes four things which appear to be essential ingredients of all effective political thinking: a finite goal, an emotional appeal, a right of moral judgment, and a ground for action."[4]

One can only conclude that Carr was a product of his time; he deplored the failure of the League of Nations and collective security yet hailed the Munich pact of Neville Chamberlain. All four points of his complaint are reasonably simple to address as we look at international politics near the end of the twentieth century. Realism as a foreign policy system functions like a reliable fire engine. It can sprinkle the neighborhood children on a hot day or it can answer a four-alarm fire. The realist caution against crusades should not be interpreted as opposition to political goals or the need for popular support of foreign policy ventures; and moral judgment, as I have interpreted it throughout this volume, is at the core of realism. Grounds for action are still primarily national interest, but they can on occasion be expanded to encompass the international community as well. A case in point was the 1990–91 war in the Persian Gulf (reemphasized in the 1998 crisis there).

In response to naked aggression on the part of Iraq in invading and occupying another sovereign state, Kuwait, the United States, as the leading international power (and with an interest in the availability of oil for its own and the international market), immediately took strenuous action. The United Nations as a whole was admirably suited to such an enterprise because in a Westphalian sense, all the members, especially the smaller nations, felt their own existence

---

4. Carr, *Twenty Years' Crisis*, 113.

might be similarly threatened if this precedent were not overcome. Although the views of the five member powers did not completely coincide, the Security Council allowed a plan to go forward to insist that Iraq withdraw under pain of UN action. So adhering to the principles of self-interest, superior power, and a moral purpose, the grand coalition sent six hundred thousand troops to the Persian Gulf and restored the status quo ante. This was a triumph for the participants and a vindication of the principles of realism. (The United States had goals beyond restoring Kuwait's freedom; these were compromised by its willingness to abide by a multilateral goal instead of the additional U.S. goal of ousting the Iraqi leader, Saddam Hussein. In this case, the United States sacrificed its own aims to the cause of the short-term world community interest. The U.S. fault here, if any, is that of its statesmen and not of realism, and the Iraq problem has continued to fester.)[5]

In brief, realism provides tools based on its three principles, and it is up to statesmen to make the proper application. The quality of the leadership of any country is tested when it decides to apply power to a political situation; what form that may take depends not only on the skill of statesmen but also on the particular circumstances. The range runs from military force through a variety of political and economic sanctions to diplomacy, or a combination of those methods. If this is so, then there is considerably more flexibility inherent in realist doctrine than a sterile repetition of events, one after the other, leading to no end and to no conclusion. Realism not only provides the glue of continuity but also assures us that the world will go on, giving us more chances in the future than some have acknowledged. Take, for example, the dangerous transition in the Kremlin.

Gorbachev in the eyes of some observers behaved in an irrational manner through the trials of *perestroika* and *glasnost*. For example, just as NATO had done in unilaterally junking tactical nuclear weapons (which were self-defeating), so did Gorbachev move on the same unilateral basis. In a recent book, former U.S. ambassador to the USSR in the early 1990s Jack Matlock retrospectively asked Gorbachev whether he moved too slowly in trying to keep the old USSR together. The response was: "Jack, I can see you are a professor now, because your question is academic. In some abstract sense, it is probably right that I moved too slowly, but I did not have the luxury of living in the abstract. I lived in a harsh world of political reality. . . . Even as it was, when I began to talk of a federation in early 1990, most of the Central Committee was in opposition. I

---

5. Robert Myers, "Ethics, Democracy and Foreign Policy: Manipulation or Participation?" *Philosophy* 13 (November–December 1991): 24–28.

had to fight them all the way. I simply did not have a free hand and should not be judged as if I did."[6]

Fortunately for humankind, Gorbachev functioned in the realist tradition, a predictive mode, and life goes on in Russia and the republics. The current leadership crisis in Russia, which is likely to continue for some time beyond the presidential term of Yeltsin, will be played out in ways that are not unfamiliar to political leaders, and the fortunes of Russia and the republics will ebb and flow along long-established channels. Now that the world regards Russian politics as being within the framework of the norms, tensions have eased, although the possibilities for crises over nuclear weapons remain.

Another problem area where realism is of enormous comfort and value in its universal pretensions is the case of China. The Chinese too are realists. The West is largely newly aware of China because of its economic success, its remarkable ability to seize and integrate the market economy into a communist political framework. This was not supposed to be possible, yet the Chinese were able to accomplish, over the past five years, production gains in GNP in the range of 11 percent per annum. This expansion has caused some economic hiccups in the United States, where China's trade surplus has already surpassed that of Japan.

This fact unsettles American business; China for a century was looked upon as a market for the United States, the "oil for the lamps of China" syndrome; but in the actual event, when the two cultures finally met again under more equal conditions of power, the reality of China became apparent, and the aphorism of the Athenians came into play: that justice can be considered only between states of equal power. This is a new experience for the United States as it faces the Pacific. It has the usual three options at first glance: the status quo, expecting China to play an accommodating role; the "primacy" role of continuing military buildup to try to contain a China that has nuclear weapons and is enlarging its armed forces; or a gradual drawing away from the western Pacific, content to maintain a military outpost in Hawaii and do as well as possible in economic affairs. There would be commerce with China, and then with the other industrialized countries. How to deal with China as the ascending power will be a preoccupation of American diplomats, scholars, and soldiers during the coming century.

One contemporary policy solution comes from a book by Richard Bernstein and Ross H. Munro, *The Coming Conflict with China.* Aside from the more bel-

---

6. Jack F. Matlock, Jr., *Autopsy on an Empire: The Ambassador's Account of the Collapse of the Soviet Union* (New York: Random House, 1995), 836.

licose and jingoistic passages promoting the idea of war with China as a self-ful-filling prophecy, there is a sound recommendation for dealing with China in the realist tradition: "The basis for any foreign policy is a clear definition of goals and a clear and consistent policy aimed at achieving those goals. There are three goals: one, to ensure peace in Asia by maintaining a stable balance of power there; two, to encourage the largest and potentially most powerful country in the region, namely China, to be a responsible state committed to nonproliferation, the peaceful resolution of disputes, and honest free trade; and three, to induce China to become more democratic and to respect the human rights of its own people, partly on the grounds that democracy and the peaceful resolution of disputes go hand in hand."[7] In an uncharacteristically pensive article, Arthur Schlesinger, Jr., wonders whether a new wave of totalitarianism may be promoted as a solution to the world's problems with malfunctioning democracy.[8]

America's putative problem with China of both tension and reconciliation may well enhance U.S. interests in trying to establish some new international regime, which may cast the United States in a more formal leadership role. It would need to look at itself in a new light. Historically, new visions of America have been provided by foreigners, seeing America for the first time, from different backgrounds and historic situations that gave a certain urgency and buoyancy to their observations. Alexis de Tocqueville visited America in 1831–1832 and wrote *Democracy in America*, celebrating the outlines of the new system of government and speculating on what they would become. In traveling down the Ohio River by steamer, for instance, he focused on the bustling activity on the northern bank and the indolence of plantation life on the southern. He saw clearly the great problems ahead for race relations. He was impressed by the vast network of private associations and their importance in building up communities governed by an energetic democratic spirit, a development totally lacking in Europe. This was the break from the European past which he proudly reported to the Western world in his book. It was the vivid contrast between the two cultures, both part of Western civilization, that gave the book its continued salience.[9]

---

7. Richard Bernstein and Ross H. Munro, *The Coming Conflict with China* (New York: Knopf, 1997), 205.

8. Arthur Schlesinger, Jr., "Has Democracy a Future?" *Foreign Affairs* 76 (September–October 1997): 2–12.

9. See Alexis de Toqueville, *Democracy in America*, ed. J. P. Meyer, trans. George Lawrence, Perennial Library Edition (New York: Harper & Row, 1969).

If *Democracy in America* foreshadowed the way democracy would grow in America, then only dimly evident to the Americans who were the participants, Max Weber's trip to America about seventy-five years later gave an early appreciation of how modern capitalism would take hold in this democratic society. The two men traveled almost identical routes, going from New York City south to the sea and then looping back. Weber was interested in how work was managed, how bureaucracies were created, and what made them operate well or poorly. He was excited by the possibilities he observed and was eager to apply his observations to his native Germany as well as other European capitalist societies.

He also watched the operation of the political system, especially the people who entered politics. He noted that in the United States, as in Germany, lawyers were heavily represented in political positions, in the whole profession of politics. This was so, he believed, because the legal profession, clustered in law firms, allowed some of the partners to participate actively in politics with no business demands on their time, against the possibility that they would find new business (today's rainmakers) or that their public prominence would reap benefits for the firm. He also noted two types of politicians, those with charisma and deep convictions, who lived for politics, and those who pursued the politics of responsibility, who operated on a lesser level and who in effect lived off politics. He saw the interconnection between bureaucracy and business and the political way of life as it was developing in the United States just before World War I.[10] People wielding power the world over were essentially the same in the context of their own societies.

The next visitor will have an equally important task but will not find it so susceptible to observation: what are the goals of the United States in regard to foreign policy? Will the American people prefer to lapse into a new isolationism, intent only on commercial interests, as President Washington recommended, or will they prefer to carry the burden in exchange for a world perhaps closer to American preferences? As is often the case in American politics, the campaign for president in the fall of 1996 failed to produce any memorable phrases or principles in regard to how America should face the world. The lack of a deontological spirit was evident. No Kantian imperative appeared as a driving force for one candidate to challenge the other in foreign policy. There seemed to be a preference for the status quo, even though it may prove transitory and impossible to maintain. American foreign policy initiatives since the

10. See John Patrick Diggins, *Max Weber: Politics and the Spirit of Tragedy* (New York: Basic Books, 1996).

Gulf War have been tentative and infrequent, which seemed to satisfy the public mood. NATO expansion and the Bosnian intervention are the most noteworthy. Yet the choice seemed to be finally that America would have to strive actively for peace, as Donald Kagan recommended, insisting that peace needs at least as careful tending as war. And as a corollary, if the peace garden is not tended, then noxious weeds of one sort or another are certain to grow, a view advanced by former secretary of state George P. Shultz.[11]

At the conclusion of his book *The Evolution of International Society,* the British scholar of international theory and politics Adam Watson, in pondering the future of international relations, lists what he sees as the available choices to shape the international community in the future. There are, according to Watson, three possibilities for establishing an authority that can create and enforce rules among states: a single power, that is, the United States; the present UN Security Council or the Group of Seven (the key industrialized nations); or some collective authority representing the world's nations, presumably some kind of super Security Council. The object of all of this is a well-ordered international system, but this is the system for the winners, for strong countries that are then obliged to deal fairly with the weak. Watson cites cases in his book of the Greek city-states and of the European system at its height, when such leadership was provided to the general satisfaction. Yet this is a fragile thing for all the reasons cited by realism: sovereign states chaff under such a hegemon, whether a benign United States or a collection of the leading powers. I noted in Chapter 8 the seventy-some proposals to modify the UN Security Council, usually centered on adding more states for reasons of power, status, and collective ego.[12]

This discussion of American foreign policy began by concentrating on the distinction between idealism and realism. Idealism can develop into sentimental desires on the part of the American people to indulge in goodwill and charity, so long as they do not jeopardize the shared national interest. Some argue that the humanitarian streak is actually in the nation's greater interest, and so it is still necessary to show concern about international disaster, natural or manmade. This attitude, however, creates a good deal of ambivalence in American foreign policy; it is not easy to be certain what the United States will do in the variety of circumstances that the troubled world creates. People think they want clear principles to follow, except that they realize the danger of unintended

---

11. See George P. Shultz, *Turmoil and Triumph: My Years as Secretary of State* (New York: Charles Scribner's Sons, 1993).

12. See Adam Watson, *The Evolution of International Society: A Comparative, Historical Analysis* (London: Routledge, 1992).

consequences; and so the ad hoc system, based on the wisdom of political realism, in the end rules. This depends, however, on the decision-making ability of
the statesman, the man who incorporates Machiavelli's *virtu* with the moral vision of the founding fathers.

The instructions of George Washington, mentioned in the Introduction, plus
the contribution of Thomas Jefferson, "that the Americans should never ask for
privileges from foreign nations in order not to grant any in return," proved to
be insufficient as permanent guides. Until World War I, foreign policy concerns
were generally on the margin, and some of the difficulty of pursuing a sound
foreign policy beyond the Washington and Jefferson caveats lay in the nature of
democracy itself: as Tocqueville wrote, "Democracy favors the growth of the
state's internal resources; it extends comfort and develops public spirit,
strengthens respect for law in the various classes of society, all of which things
have no more than an indirect influence on the standing of one nation in respect to another."[13] Tocqueville dealt with other problems endemic to democracy and foreign policy—the difficulty of keeping secrets, for example—but the
primacy of domestic over foreign policy is the one most difficult to resolve, unless—and ideally—one can see the direct link between a domestic imperative
and a supporting foreign policy role. Strong domestic interests are the best
guide to long-term foreign policy goals. As America has become a trading nation since the end of World War II, it has been possible to find and rally support
for "free trade" on an international basis. The United States both promoted
and joined the World Trade Organization (WTO) through the UN. There is an
ongoing series of agreements and protocols as well with our leading trading
partners, such as Japan and Mexico. The North American Free Trade Association (NAFTA) may not fully meet the hopes of its sponsor because in an economy and market as diverse as that of the United States, different sectors and regions in agriculture, manufacturing, and so on cannot be served equally. Broom
makers in Missouri are pressed to the wall by Mexican competition.

On the other hand, the demands of modern finance in terms of banking,
brokerage, and insurance clearly have worldwide implications, and those countries that prefer to stand by their basic mercantilist purposes (despite their
membership in the WTO), Japan, Korea, and Switzerland, for example, are
fighting a losing battle. Many recent developments in the economic field might
have in the nineteenth century provided the tinderbox for a world conflagra-
tion, but nowadays such problems are handled by the fire extinguishers of di-

13. Tocqueville, *Democracy in America*, 229.

plomacy. The Asian financial crises of the late 1990s strained but did not break the world financial system.

Yet the future of war and peace in the twenty-first century defies the standard crystal ball. There are two main lines of prediction. One is about what the United States will do. Because the United States still produces about 25 percent of the world's economic output, its economy cannot be ignored in the global marketplace, and its military superiority makes it a factor to be reckoned with in any global eruption, large or small. There have been arguments concerning America's relative position of strength and weakness, but the decline myth, popular in the 1980s, has been slow to materialize.[14] If world politics continues more or less as it has in the past, the American position will determine the outline of international relations in the twenty-first century.

The principal alternative is some version of Huntington's "clash of civilizations." "Possible international futures all miss a new dynamic point . . . all miss a crucial, indeed a central, aspect of what global politics is likely to be in the coming years."[15] In this article, Huntington sees the old divisions of nations into first, second, and third worlds as no longer valid; the operative units, unwieldy as they seem, will rather be the world's great civilizations, organized along cultural lines instead of by state. Huntington thus distinguishes among eight world civilizations—Western, Confucian, Japanese, Islamic, Hindu, Slavic-Orthodox, Latin American, and possibly African. The great clashes of the future, he claims, will be along the "fault" lines of these loose entities. The differences among these civilization groups are basic, perduring, and not subject to glossing over.

Such grand theories of international affairs, like Arnold Toynbee's *Study of History,* are awe-inspiring in their scholarship, in the concept of challenge and response, but are not of much help in dealing with current and specific conflicts.[16] The conflicts Huntington is concerned with largely involve Bosnia, Iran, Iraq, the African turmoil, struggles inside the former Soviet Union, and especially the danger of a crusading Islam. The insights provided by such theories are something one should be aware of, but they are not likely to be at the forefront of the statesman's agenda. They in no way challenge the realist paradigm.

14. See Henry R. Nau, *The Myth of America's Decline: Leading the World Economy into the 1990s* (New York: Oxford University Press, 1990).

15. Huntington, "The Clash of Civilizations?" 22. Huntington later expanded this article into a book of the same title.

16. Arnold Toynbee, *A Study of History* (New York: Oxford University Press, 1947).

More immediate, great-power potential conflicts might occur between China and the United States. Civilizational factors certainly would be in play, but basic hostility would likely be expressed in the tradition of rival national states. It is a current mantra of international disputes that because of alleged historic forces leading all nations toward democracy (Fukuyama's book *The End of History and the Last Man*, based on the Hegelian world spirit leading toward liberal democracy, was an earlier indicator of this thesis), disputes between China and the United States and other threatening situations will be resolved peacefully. Some predict that China will be democratic by 2005.[17] Larry Diamond is more broadly optimistic. He predicts, "At some point in the first two decades of the twenty-first century—as economic development transforms the societies of East Asia in particular—the world will then be poised for a 'fourth wave' of democratization, and quite possibly a boon to international peace and security far more profound and enduring than we have seen with the end of the Cold War."[18]

Other areas of international dispute apparently no longer have the capability to excite international threats because they do not challenge any significant balance of power. This seems especially true of the economic plight of the poverty-stricken countries of the world, particularly in Africa, Southeast Asia, and Latin America. In the 1970s and 1980s during the height of the Cold War, the Third World and nonaligned nations had a claim on both superpowers that amounted to a willingness to accept aid and arms from both sides against a pledge not to join either camp. This was the era of the "Group of 77," which actually included over 120 members of the UN General Assembly. This group insisted on a "new economic order," a "new information order," or, in other words, a realignment of wealth and power as a right.

As this period began, Stanley Hoffmann dealt with some of the implications in his book *Duties beyond Borders*. "What are we, as citizens or governments of the richest countries, obligated to do?" He outlines three positions—minimalist, maximalist, and a middle position. "The minimalist position consists in saying that we have no duties towards states or people other than our own. In other words, it may be a matter of self-interest or prudence or charity to watch over conditions in the rest of the world but it is not a matter of moral obligations; even if the ultimate scandal is the plight of individuals in three-fourths of

17. See Henry Rowen, "The Short March: China's Road to Democracy," *National Interest,* Spring 1996, 61–70.

18. Larry Diamond, "Is the Third Wave Over?" *Journal of Democracy* 7 (July 1996): 20–31.

the world, there is no duty."[19] There is in any case no obligation of justice among states, only among individuals. And if stronger states transferred wealth and power to weak states, there would be immediate chaos and the end of order. This is the attitude of the world toward North Korea, for example, where about 15 percent of the population at one point was reportedly dying of starvation.[20]

The maximalist argument claims an obligation to all of mankind: "To put it bluntly, our obligation of justice toward the Bantus is exactly the same as our obligation of justice toward our immediate neighbors." Such a claim, Hoffmann concedes, is exceptionally difficult to maintain in the real world, although, despite so many violations of human rights in the world, "one can support the idea that human beings should be treated as having the same moral standing." This argument remains the goal of our human rights conventions, but in the contemporary world, a "somewhere in between" position on distributive justice, though flawed, holds sway.[21] John Rawls, in his book *A Theory of Justice,* advocates an egalitarian theory to approach the ideal of equal treatment and resource allocation; he claims that representatives of a society (not voting as representatives of their own particular interest) should meet behind a "veil of ignorance" so that in dividing up society's assets, no one would know what his own share would be.[22] This has no clear implications for international relations, although Charles Beitz tries to extend the idea in his *Theory of International Relations.* Fairness is the moral claim for egalitarian distribution of community-produced wealth.

All such efforts to create a world that does not exist (to paraphrase Machiavelli) have serious limitations in both domestic and international politics. They pose particular problems for the United States as it tries to do good at home and fulfill a set of self-imposed obligations that it promotes to bring order and prosperity to a tumultuous world. It is likely that the United States, in one of the possibilities set forth by Adam Watson (as real-world alternatives to worldwide democracy and clashing civilizations), will be called upon to take international leadership, as it often does. This is the main conclusion of a book by Joseph S. Nye, Jr., director of the International Security Agency of the Pentagon

19. Stanley Hoffmann, *Duties beyond Borders: On the Limits and Possibilities of Ethical International Politics* (Syracuse: Syracuse University Press, 1981), 151.

20. See *New York Times,* 15 September 1997.

21. Hoffmann, *Duties beyond Borders,* 153.

22. John Rawls, *A Theory of Justice* (Cambridge, Mass.: Belknap Press of Harvard University Press, 1971).

in the first Clinton administration and now head of the Kennedy Center at Harvard University. Writing in 1990, he stressed that the United States has both the military power (hard power) and economic power (soft power) to make the world system of interdependence a success. This would require a massive and selfless effort supported by the American people to build institutions and approach the world with an "open attitude: to make this new world work. The corollary is a strong domestic program that provides both the resources and the commitment to such a global task."[23]

Others see "security communities" assembling, particularly in Europe, where common interests and ideas may lead to the formation of blocs of peace-loving states, based on shared democratic values. This is the official policy of America, "expanding" democratic possibilities everywhere, in a new Hegelian inspiration. Presumably other blocs of states could also build communities, based on different, perhaps nondemocratic, values, although the preferences and expectations of "wave theorists" would be disappointed if not confounded. Still, such blocs based on authoritarian values could challenge both democratic blocs and civilization enclaves, if those are indeed forming.

Yet despite these favorable developments (and counterdevelopments) and the hopes that always seem to accompany the prospect of dramatic change, is there really any reason to expect such a denial of history as a world totally committed to peace? Kagan earlier emphasized that if peace is to be maintained, there must be a steady and serious effort to accomplish that goal. The same national enthusiasm and willingness to sacrifice must arise in the cause of peace as in the cause of war. So far, there is little evidence of that desideratum.

This option for peace is certainly much to be hoped for and attempted, going beyond the present efforts of regional groups, which are basically functional groupings, as well as the UN mechanism. But what are the golden apples of discord that would reactivate Thucydides' warning that wars arise from questions of "honor, fear, and interest"? Will questions about the present distribution of the world's resources, e.g., oil, lend themselves to easy resolution if the status quo is altered by conflictual demands and expectations of different amalgams of power? Natural resources (always subject to greed and envy) to one side, do questions of honor and fear automatically disappear in a peaceful world where America leads and its ideas and values prevail? There is no indication that wars over religion and ethnicity have lost their historical appeal, whether inside, outside, or between civilizational blocs.

---

23. Joseph S. Nye, Jr., *Bound to Lead: The Changing Nature of American Power* (New York: Basic Books, 1990), 260–61.

Or, on another level, is it a matter of indifference to Americans who is in charge of the contemporary world, if in fact anyone can exercise a hegemonic role? Here again Huntington has advice to offer; he extols the virtues of American "primacy" on the grounds not only that it is a good thing for global order and progress but that there are many advantages as to whose values and preferences prevail.[24] Arguments familiar after the Vietnam War as to whether America was a force for good or evil in the world appear to have been resolved after the Cold War victory in favor of American rectitude and virtue and the conclusion that its leadership in the world community is on balance a positive force. Yet we cannot take this for granted. As William Pfaff writes, "The exercise of traditional moral and political responsibility is never a settled matter—as it is not in life itself."[25]

The next century perhaps holds a new, bright future for the United States as well as the rest of the world, free of the darkness of the twentieth century, the most savage century in history. Interest, power, and morality cannot do more than rationalize and make the best of whatever security problem arises. The comfort in this is that the decision-making process is placed in our own hands—not on automatic pilot— and issues can be resolved with a bias toward justice, in the sense that the legitimate concerns of all parties are considered and answered as far as possible. Realism insists that we are responsible for our actions, and therein lie our best prospects for coping with national interests and global responsibilities. A version of Kant's republic or Western democracy may reveal unexpected possibilities for conflict resolution. If so, there may be fewer occasions for the permanent dark side of the human animal to show its fangs. But if the occasion for war is lessened, there is no reason to think that it will lose its intensity, as the twentieth century has shown. There is nothing in that formula that guarantees a new golden age. It does, however, assure us, through the realist experience, of a proven way to make the best of what situations the human race is likely to experience. For a great antiwar counterforce to arise to head off aggression would only demonstrate its failure. The better realism is understood, the more likely its leading practitioners will be required to act virtuously in public, which may hold their worst tendencies in check.

Appeals to justice will continue to be heard; every war will be a "just war." The calculation of consequences will become refined enough, one might expect,

---

24. Samuel Huntington, "Why International Primacy Matters," *International Security* 17 (Spring 1993): 68–83.

25. William Pfaff, "The Future of the United States as a Great Power" (Carnegie Council on Ethics and International Affairs, 1995).

so that not going to war may clearly be in everyone's self-interest, as the long nuclear truce so far has demonstrated. America will presumably continue to stand on that side, making its preference for peace heard but knowing that it might become the victim of its own ego and self-righteousness. One can aspire to choose the lesser evil, according to political realism the best choice available, knowing that it may well prolong the possibilities for peace into and through the twenty-first century.

Selected Annotated Bibliography

For those interested in consulting in more detail the essential sources of this volume, the following books are suggested for additional reading.

Bury, J. B. *The Idea of Progress: An Inquiry into Its Origin and Growth.* 1920; New York: Dover, 1987. Introduction by Charles Beard. This is the classic work on the importance of this thesis for Western civilization. The idea persists to this day, with various consequences.

Butterfield, Herbert. *The Statecraft of Machiavelli.* New York: Collier Books, 1960. Butterfield, the great British Christian realist, deals charitably with the subject and concentrates in particular on Machiavelli's historiography.

Carr, E. H. *The Twenty Years' Crisis, 1919–1939: An Introduction to the Study of International Relations.* London: Macmillan, 1942. This classic realist critique of the legalistic talk that characterized the interwar years, leaving the European allies ill prepared for the Axis, is flawed by the author's embrace of Munich.

Donnelly, Jack. *Universal Human Rights in Theory and Practice.* Ithaca: Cornell University Press, 1989. One of the early influential writers on the importance of including human rights in universal assertions, Donnelly anticipated many of the current arguments on relativism.

Fairbank, John K., Edwin O. Reischauer, and Albert M. Craig. *East Asia: Tradition and Transformation.* Boston: Houghton Mifflin, 1973. This is the authoritative text of the structure of classic Chinese civilization and its fateful encounter with the West in the nineteenth and twentieth centuries.

Fukuyama, Francis. *The End of History and the Last Man.* New York: Free Press, 1992. This is a daring attempt to explain the advance of democracy in modern times in terms of Hegelian philosophy. The end of history is the creation worldwide of liberal democratic governments, a dubious but challenging theory.

Gordon, Wendell. *The United Nations at the Crossroads of Reform.* London: M. E. Sharpe, 1994. This book is typical of a category of structural approaches to world organization that in effect call for world government in the name of strengthening the United Nations.

Green, Donald P., and Ian Shapiro. *Pathologies of Rational Choice Theory: A Critique of Applications in Political Science.* New Haven: Yale University Press, 1994. This book is an excellent rejoinder to the claim of rational choice theory to be the scientific answer to questions in all fields of the social sciences.

Hardin, Russell. *One for All: The Logic of Group Conflict.* Princeton: Princeton University Press, 1995. This book raises issues that, in microcosm, parallel those encountered in international relations, for example, whether it may be wiser to pursue individual interests rather than group interests as a better way to achieve community.

Hobsbawm, Eric. *The Age of Extremes: A History of the World, 1914–1991.* New York: Pantheon, 1994. This is a researched reminiscence of a fine historian looking back over his own life in the twentieth century, pausing to interpret the great events of those times. He concentrates on the wars and the ideologies behind them.

Hoffmann, Stanley. *Duties beyond Borders: On the Limits and Possibilities of Ethical International Politics.* Syracuse: Syracuse University Press, 1981. Hoffmann's lecture series at Syracuse University dealing with international responsibilities and national interests remains critical to our understanding of modern concerns over such issues as humanitarian intervention.

Hoge, James F., and Fareed Zakaria, eds. *The American Encounter: The United States and the Making of the Modern World.* New York: Basic Books, 1997. The editors have assembled many of the central primary texts—from the pages of *Foreign Affairs*—that document America's rise to globalism. One need not strain too much to see how this rising superpower sought to build an international system according to its own values and in its own image. The results for the nation and the world are mixed, and "progress" is neither self-evident nor linear.

Huntington, Samuel P. *The Clash of Civilizations and the Remaking of World Order.* New York: Simon & Schuster, 1996. Seeking new explanations for the parlous condition of the world and dissatisfied with the future of the sovereign state system, Huntington seeks a new way to explain future world crises based on "civilization fault lines."

———. *The Third Wave: Democratization in the Late Twentieth Century.* Norman: University of Oklahoma Press, 1991. This is one of the books that has helped to popularize the alleged triumph of democracy over its competitors in the twentieth century. Can the fourth wave be far behind?

Johnson, James Turner. *Can Modern War Be Just?* New Haven: Yale University Press, 1984. While Johnson has some difficulty literally taking the criteria of the just war rules of antiquity into the modern age, he nonetheless stays loyally with the tradition, even though it requires considerable adroitness and acrobatic skill.

Johnston, Alastair Ian. *Cultural Realism: Strategic Culture and Grand Strategy in Chinese History.* Princeton: Princeton University Press, 1997. Johnston performs a great service by bringing Chinese military methods and perceptions, not just gongs and cymbals, into the world of balance-of-power politics.

Kagan, Donald. *On the Origins of War and the Preservation of Peace*. New York: Double-day, 1995. While impressed by the persistence of war in world history, Kagan nonetheless is optimistic. If mankind would work as hard to preserve peace as to wage war, a more compassionate world might find peace in our time.

Kant, Immanuel. *Perpetual Peace: A Philosophical Essay*. Written in 1795, this book can be found in English translation in most libraries. I own a 1915 reprint of a 1903 edition, which I quoted from. A more available translation is *Kant: Political Writings*, edited by Hans Reis, 2d enlarged ed. Cambridge: Cambridge University Press, 1991.

Kegley, Charles W., Jr., ed. *Controversies in International Relations Theory: Realism and the Neoliberal Challenge*. New York: St. Martin's Press, 1985. This is a fair sampling of the various ways international relations academics look at the perennial arguments between realists and idealists, adding a new line of neo-considerations.

Keohane, Robert O. *Neorealism and Its Critics*. New York: Columbia University Press, 1986. Among those critical of existing ways of looking at international relations, Keohane was a leader in regime theory and various neo-propositions analyzing international politics from new perspectives.

Kissinger, Henry. *Diplomacy*. New York: Simon & Schuster, 1994. This is a brilliant account of the long tradition of Western diplomacy, concentrating on the twentieth century, when Kissinger played a pivotal role in the late 1960s and 1970s. His style was the balance of power, aimed at preserving the status quo to America's benefit.

Lebow, Richard Ned, and Thomas Reese-Kappen. *International Relations Theory and the End of the Cold War*. New York: Columbia University Press, 1995. Contributors to this volume in general are eager to promote new notions of how international relations should work after the end of confrontation with the Soviet Union. Lebow, for example, believes that realism has failed.

McDougall, Walter A. *Promised Land, Crusader State: The American Encounter with the World since 1776*. Boston: Houghton Mifflin, 1997. It has been said that U.S. foreign policy is "one part strategy, one part liturgy." This book explains the historical reasons for this dichotomy, destroying numerous myths about American exceptionalism along the way. After reading it, one cannot help but recognize the continuing relevance of realism, correctly interpreted as a triad of elements that encompass morality, reason, and power.

McNamara, Robert S. *In Retrospect: The Tragedy and Lessons of Vietnam*. New York: Random House, 1995. While the book is in part self-serving—an elaborate explanation of the complex circumstances that might have confused any secretary of defense—there are keen and critical insights into top-level mishandling of the Vietnam War that make it well worth reading.

Machiavelli, Niccolò. *The Discourses on Livy*. London: Penguin, 1983. Written concurrently with *The Prince*, this book is a more leisurely account of the leading historical personalities in antiquity who Machiavelli thinks are worthy of emulation. This is a good example of the inductive method of historical scholarship that Machiavelli uses.

————. *The Prince.* London: Penguin, 1995. This thin volume outlines Machiavelli's unvarnished advice, written in 1513 and 1514, on how the then-contemporary prince is to obtain and hold power. Reading commentaries for a sense of the times moderates the amorality of some of Machiavelli words.

MacIntyre, Alasdair. *After Virtue: A Study in Moral Theory.* Notre Dame: Notre Dame University Press, 1981. This is a philosophical attack on the "barbarians at the gate." MacIntyre insists that the modern world has abandoned dependable classicists such as Plato, with his universal assumptions, and substituted modern relativism, or emotivism, where everyone is on his own.

Manent, Pierre. *An Intellectual History of Liberalism,* trans. Rebecca Balinski. Princeton: Princeton University Press, 1994. This book makes a powerful modern case that the centuries-old conflict between church and state in modern Europe continues in contemporary politics. The key issue of who is in charge—the king or the bishop—remains. The struggle for power continues.

Mansfield, Harvey C. *Machiavelli's Virtue.* Chicago: University of Chicago Press, 1996. This is an attempt by an outstanding political philosopher to project the work of Machiavelli into the modern era. Claims are made for the relevance of Machiavelli's thought, making him a modern-day Confucius, whose destiny is not for himself to rule but to supply the ideas and techniques of power for the powers that be.

Morgenthau, Hans J. *Politics among Nations: The Struggle for Power and Peace.* 3d ed. New York: Knopf, 1960. This book is discussed extensively at the beginning of this text. The year 1998 marked the fiftieth anniversary of the publication of the first edition. The last, "brief" edition was edited by Kenneth W. Thompson in 1993. Over half a million copies of *Politics among Nations* have been sold, demonstrating its impact on American academic life over five decades.

————. *Scientific Man vs. Power Politics.* Chicago: University of Chicago Press, 1946. This is probably Morgenthau's most seminal book. It provides the philosophical base for his realist political philosophy as applied to international relations. Morgenthau shows that the scientific method works for the natural and physical sciences but not for the social sciences. This remains a fundamental argument.

————. *Truth and Power: Essays of a Decade, 1960–70.* New York: Praeger, 1970. This is a collection of essays written by Morgenthau in a pensive, reflective mood during the Vietnam War. He had expected the government to follow his advice on avoiding the folly of this war; instead, he was added to the "enemies" list.

Nelson, M. Frederick. *Korea and the Old Orders in Eastern Asia.* Baton Rouge: Louisiana State University Press, 1945. This is a pathfinding account of the old Chinese tributary system as applied to the ancient state of Korea. This background is still important to understanding the security situation in Northeast Asia.

Neufield, Mark A. *The Restructuring of International Relations Theory.* New York: Cambridge University Press, 1995. Of particular interest in this serious and determined book is the treatment of the rise and fall of positivism as a social science theory, of its misguided and finally failed efforts to wrap up all scientific knowledge—including "social science"—in a single explanation.

Phillips, Robert L. *War and Justice.* Norman: University of Oklahoma Press, 1984. This is an exceptionally balanced treatment of the origin of the just war tradition, laying heavy emphasis on the role of the Catholic Church in promoting the theory, as a way both to lessen bloodshed in the Dark Ages and to maintain its seat at the tables of political power.

Plutarch. *The Rise and Fall of Athens: Nine Greek Lives.* London: Penguin, 1960. This account of some of the leading personalities of this age of antiquity is a valuable contribution to a study of the times but particularly for an appreciation of the Peloponnesian War. The portraits of Pericles and Alcibiades are especially recommended.

Popper, Karl. *The Poverty of Historicism.* London: Routledge, 1991. This book was first published in three parts in 1944 and 1945. It is an angry but penetrating critique of the perils of both the fascist and communist philosophies, which insist on a particular interpretation of history and the inevitability of foreordained results.

Rosenthal, Joel H. *Righteous Realists: Political Realism, Responsible Power, and American Culture in the Nuclear Age.* Baton Rouge: Louisiana State University Press, 1991. This book focuses on the leading American realist political thinkers of this century—Kennan, Morgenthau, Niebuhr, Lippmann—and their contribution to the principles of American foreign policy. All had to deal with the relationship between ethics and politics.

Smith, Michael Joseph. *Realism from Weber to Kissinger.* Baton Rouge: Louisiana State University Press, 1986. This work is a critical consideration of a long sweep of Western political thinkers presented by those writing in the realist tradition. In the author's view, the flaws in realist philosophy outweigh the strengths.

Strauss, Leo, and Joseph Cropsey, eds. *History of Political Philosophy.* 3d ed. Chicago: University of Chicago Press, 1987. This is the standard and invaluable reference on the subject. Among the essays, the one on Machiavelli by Leo Strauss is exceptional.

Thompson, Kenneth W. *Community, Diversity, and the New World Order.* Lanham, Md.: University Press of America, 1994. This is another in the long series of books and essays by Kenneth Thompson that demonstrate the practical steps required for a more peaceful and successful world. High among them are the appreciation of the nature of power and the role of morality in making the world order work.

Thucydides. *On Justice, Power and Human Nature: The Essence of Thucydides' History of the Peloponnesian War.* Edited and translated by Paul Woodruff. Indianapolis: Hackett, 1993. This is a much-acclaimed selection from the Greek historian Thucydides' account of the war and the events surrounding it. Woodruff's notes hold it together nicely.

Tucker, Robert W. *The Just War: A Study in Contemporary American Doctrine.* Baltimore: Johns Hopkins University Press, 1960. The tone of this book is skeptical of the morality of the just war doctrine and sees within it the seeds of self-delusion and self-serving that became all too obvious in the Vietnam War.

Walzer, Michael. *Just and Unjust Wars: A Moral Argument with Historical Illustrations.* New York: Basic Books, 1977. A preface to the second edition, 1992, concerns the Gulf

War. This is the quintessential account of how one should think about the question of war. It is a balanced work of scholarship, if one can accept the premise uncritically.

Wight, Martin. *International Theory: The Three Traditions.* New York: Holmes & Meier, 1992. This is a collection of lectures by the late Martin Wight assembled by his students. Here we find his well-known division of international relations theorists into rationalists, realists, and revolutionaries. The book contains valuable material, whether or not this tripartite distinction is important.

INDEX